Baptists have often … en ignoring the Lord's Su… in life, and there has s… …ence that such an accusation has merit. Thus, it is good to be able to recommend this book in which Baptist pastor and theologian, Richard Barcellos, reclaims the Lord's Supper as a means of grace and argues for its significance in the life of the local congregation. It is to be hoped that this book will have a significant influence in encouraging us all to think more carefully about the role of the Supper in the life of our churches.

Carl R. Trueman,
Paul Woolley Professor of Church History,
Westminster Theological Seminary, Philadelphia, Pennsylvania

Ever since the mid-nineteenth century, evangelical eucharistic theology and praxis have been marred by a deep-seated anemia. The origins of this condition are manifold, but surely one of them is the lack of a robust view of the spiritual presence of Christ at his table. In this regard, Richard Barcellos is to be commended heartily for detailing the biblical and theological foundations of what our forefathers in the faith knew well, namely, that, the Lord's table is, in the words of the Calvinistic Baptist William Kiffin, a vehicle of "spiritual nourishment."

Michael A. G. Haykin,
Professor of Church History and Biblical Spirituality,
The Southern Baptist Theological Seminary, Louisville, Kentucky

There are at least three qualities that combine for the making of good "stewards of the mysteries of God": skill in the interpretation of Scripture, familiarity with the history of Christian thought (for perspective, insight and the detection of error), and acquaintance with the human heart for the due application ("rightly dividing") of scriptural truth. In his newest book Richard Barcellos brings out these qualities for the task of helping his fellow stewards appreciate and dispense the rich fare of the Lord's Supper.

The book provides a greatly needed exegetically demonstrated answer to the question, "What is the meaning of the Lord's Supper?" For many, it is a mere memorial. A memorial does not need to be thought of as "mere". In fact, memorials of God's redemptive acts, may, as such, be a powerful means of grace if used correctly, but for many, even as such its value is lost. The greatest strength of Dr. Barcellos' book is his exegetical demonstration that the Supper is so much more than a memorial; it is a God-given way for the actual experience of, a participation in, a true, real, spiritual "eating" of the glorified Christ, with the result of a true increase of spiritual joy, strength, and growth in the likeness of the Lord. Along with this, he corrects several serious doctrinal and practical errors which have come into the church and which have kept the children of God from rightly and fully receiving the blood-bought benefits of the sacred meal. Here is the old Reformed doctrine of the Supper, a truth for which Protestants were martyred, the doctrine set forth in all Reformed Confessions, set forth afresh and convincingly to twenty-first century readers, soundly proven and extensively explained from the Holy Scriptures. Written with students in mind, it should be on the required reading list of all who are preparing to be ministers of the Word.

Richard W. Daniels,
Author of *The Christology of John Owen*

The Lord's Supper is more than a memory. Modern Baptists have often fallen into the "dead memorial" category. Others have emphasized self-examination to the point of morbidity. Our Particular Baptist forefathers taught the "spiritual presence of Christ" in the supper, and an understanding of this is vital to our spiritual vitality. This new book by Dr. Barcellos will be a great help for men in the ministry, and those studying for the ministry.

May God use this book as a catalyst in bringing about continuing reform in our churches.

Steve Marquedant,
Pastor, Sovereign Grace Baptist Church, Ontario, California

None of us have fully appreciated the stupendous blessing which the Lord's Supper is to Christ's church, but Dr. Barcellos' excellent treatment of this subject can strengthen our grasp upon the exalted reality. With capable exegesis of key Scripture passages, demonstrable consistency with the best systematic theology, and informed interaction with historic Christian thought, this important work will, with God's blessing, assist modern pastors to realize better the true nature of this second ordinance of Christ as a capacious channel of sanctifying grace. With unqualified recommendation I urge a careful reading of this book, especially if your theologically formative influences were similar to mine, committed to the memorial view of the Supper, not unusual among Baptists of the last century or so.

An especially delightful surprise awaits the reader at the end, where Dr. Barcellos cogently links the profound spiritual realities he has proven from Scripture with the most practical implications for the manner of Lord's Supper observance in our churches. The connection of doctrine and practice in this area may not have been obvious at first, but having seen it in print, I find it inescapable. May the Lord reform his churches and strengthen our unity by the standard of his Word and through the sound teaching of this incisive analysis.

D. Scott Meadows,
Pastor, Calvary Baptist Church (Reformed), Exeter, New Hampshire

I warmly recommend this modern presentation of the Reformed or Calvinistic doctrine of the Lord's Supper. The contents of the book demonstrate the aptness of its title. It is founded on a thorough exposition of Scripture, with particular attention to the teaching of the apostle Paul and it is consistent with the great Reformation confessions of faith. Some treatments of this position have tended to be abstruse: this is not. It demands careful attention as all scriptural doctrines do, but the careful reader will find it warm and practical. Many Christians have adopted a memorialist view in reaction to the false sacramentalism promoted in some quarters. Richard Barcellos calls us back to the biblical position of our fathers. Such a return can only enrich the worship of our churches and that of individual members. Thoroughly practical it deserves a wide sale and careful study.

Robert W. Oliver,
Bradford on Avon, UK
Visiting Professor of Church History,
Puritan Reformed Seminary, Grand Rapids, Michigan,
Author of *History of the English Calvinistic Baptists 1771-1892*

The Lord's Supper as a Means of Grace

The Lord's Supper as a Means of Grace

More than a memory

Richard C. Barcellos

MENTOR

ISBN 978-1-78191-268-3 – Book
ISBN 978-1-78191-312-3 – ePub
ISBN 978-1-78191-313-0 – Mobi

Published in 2013
in the
Mentor Imprint
by
Christian Focus Publications,
Geanies House, Fearn, Ross-shire,
IV20 1TW, Scotland.

www.christianfocus.com

Cover design by Daniel Van Straaten

Printed and bound by Bell and Bain, Glasgow

MIX
Paper from responsible sources
FSC www.fsc.org FSC® C007785

Contents

Foreword 11

Preface 15

Introduction 21

1. The Terminology connected to the Lord's Supper in the New Testament 31
2. Communion at the Lord's Supper 41
3. Spiritual Blessings and the Holy Spirit 55
4. Spiritual Invigoration through Prayer 73
5. The Confessional and Catechetical Formulation of the Lord's Supper as a Means of Grace in the Reformed Creedal Tradition 87
6. Final Thoughts 103

Bibliography 115

Name andSubject Index 121

Scripture Index 127

Foreword

It is a curious fact that the most difficult issue under debate during the era of the Reformation was not Justification by Faith alone or even the place of the Papacy in the church. It was rather the theology and practice of the Lord's Supper. Lives were lost, much blood was shed and potential alliances failed because of differences over eucharistic observance. Romanists, Lutherans, the Swiss and the English reformers all debated the question at length. While they did not always agree, the very fact that this question was central in the minds of reformation-era theologians ought to cause us to reflect on its importance. We should learn at least one thing from this: the Lord's Supper was no small matter in the eyes of these theologians and pastors, and for that reason (among many others), it ought to be equally important to their heirs.

Can this be said of the twenty-first century church? Hardly. While the practice of baptism still divides Christians into two camps, the theology and practice of the Table of the Lord seldom creates even a stir. It has been pushed into the background by a host of influences.

Very few consider its purpose in the divine plan, its usefulness in the church, or its place in the life of the believer. One wonders, 'why do churches observe the Supper?' In some, it is nothing more than a tradition—something passed from generation to generation as a venerated religious custom. Others recognize that it has an evident importance, but only at times of perceived necessity, observing it on special occasions, usually at lengthy intervals. In certain cases, it is ignored or rejected as an antiquated rite. I once visited a mega-church where the elements were placed on three or four tables scattered around the auditorium, with a notice in the bulletin that if anyone felt the need of observing the Supper, they were free to do so on a self-serve basis! Sadly, we might fairly characterize most churches and Christians today as indifferent to the Supper.

Who is right? While we may not wish to return to the days of debate and division, we must say that our Reformation fathers had a far better understanding of the place and importance of this observance than do most ministers and believers today. They recognized that it was a divinely instituted practice, given to the church for great benefit. As such, it deserved careful, close examination and definition. For this reason, we also need to give thoughtful consideration to both the theology and practice of the Supper. Dr. Barcellos has given that to us in the book you are holding.

This work combines close exegesis, sound biblical-theological conclusions, key insights from Systematic Theology and respect for the work of the Spirit of Christ in the history of the church in order to reach its conclusions. All of these deserve a part in our thinking, and each makes significant contributions to our conclusions. Careful examination of the Word of God is the proper place to begin. Our primary standard governs all that we do and say, and calls us to re-order our doctrine and practice to conform to its dictates. Biblical theology teaches us about the redeeming purposes of God in Christ, and about our relationship to those things accomplished by our Lord.

How does He now, in this age between His advents, dispense grace to His people? Systematic theology brings together various strands of truth, describing God's purpose in giving the sacraments, and historical theology teaches us how others have understood the same texts of Scripture, and ensures that we do not pursue novelties. Each of these comes together in this book, showing us how a sovereign God fulfills his covenant promises in an orderly and ordinary way.

We also live in an era in which there is a great clamor for the influence of the Holy Spirit, and this is usually defined in terms of the visible, sensible and audible. The largest 'churches' in most cities around the world are those that claim to perform miracles, signs and wonders; preachers tout experiences of various kinds—frequently of the ecstatic variety; and even many evangelicals have abandoned a dependence on the Spirit's voice in the written Word of God for dubious claims of continuing revelation. Richard Barcellos shows us here that the Holy Spirit of God brings grace to His people through the channels He has established. These are churchly channels. In this case, the focus is on the Supper (and prayer in its relationship with the Supper) but there are clear references as well to the importance of the preached word and baptism. The crying need of the hour is a return to these unspectacular but divinely appointed instruments in the hands of the divine redeemer.

But the observance of the Lord's Supper has pastoral and practical applications as well. In the final chapter of this book, Dr. Barcellos provides some very encouraging advice for churches. He has not simply repeated traditional evangelical exhortations, but has suggested some very helpful and necessary correctives to those traditions, based in careful readings of the text of Scripture.

This book will make you think. For too long Christians have been content with an accepted practice that reflects, not so much Scripture (though there are echoes of God's revelation in it), but more an individualistic piety devoid of the Spirit's influence. They practice an outward form of godliness but deny its power. The true work of the

Holy Spirit now is neither in the miraculous gifts nor in some form of continuing revelation. It is in the means of grace, conforming us more and more into the image of our blessed Savior.

Perhaps the words of two esteemed godly ministers from the past may summarize the matter for us. Thomas Goodwin said:

> The whole edification of every saint, by the means of grace, which are the ordinances and other means whatsoever, all flow from the benign influences of this Spirit accompanying them, and bedewing men's hearts by them. And for the proof of this in general, you have that passage, Acts ix. 31, 'Then had the churches rest, and *were edified*, walking in the fear of the Lord.' And so it is said of churches walking in all the order and ordinances of Christ; as of the Colossian church it is spoken (chap, ii.) that they did so; 'in the comfort of the Holy Ghost,' as the author of that edification and comfort by those ordinances. (*The Works of Thomas Goodwin*, 6:36-37)

And the greatest English speaking theologian, John Owen, wrote this:

> Such is the nature of the unalterable decree of God in this matter, that no person living can ever attain the end of glory and happiness without the means of grace and holiness; the same eternal purpose respecteth both. (*The Works of John Owen*, 3:592-93)

Read this book, and then enjoy the blessings of the Lords Supper with your church, to the glory of God.

James M. Renihan, Ph.D.
Dean, Professor of Historical Theology
Institute of Reformed Baptist Studies
At Westminster Seminary California
Escondido, CA

Preface

This book has come as a result of two primary contributing factors. First, I was asked to address the issue of the Lord's Supper as a means of grace at the General Assembly of the Association of Reformed Baptist Churches of America in the spring of 2011. That request came to me at a time in my life when I could devote extra thought to this worthy subject. Some of my more refined conclusions have come as a result of this. The other and more important contributing factor is that I am a pastor and have been since 1990 (except for a brief period in the mid-2000s). Over the years I had given sporadic thought to the Lord's Supper as a means of grace but never nailed down some important specifics – namely, not only that, but *how*, the Lord's Supper is a means of grace. The material that follows is a pastor's attempt at showing how the Supper is a means of grace. It comprises some of the major exegetical and theological issues I had to work through to understand better the Bible's teaching as well as understanding the confessional and catechetical formulation of the Reformed tradition. Though it involves answering questions I had on this subject, I have found that others often have these same questions.

The book is not an exhaustive treatment of the Lord's Supper. It has a primary focus that can be stated in question format. *How is the Lord's Supper a means of grace?* I do not deal with many important issues related to the Supper, nor do I interact with all the secondary historical-theological issues and sources. My aim is very specific – to provide exegetical and theological grounds upon which the Supper is seen as a means of grace. I will also examine some of the Reformed tradition's confessions and catechisms. That part of the study seeks to illustrate how the exegetical and theological data has been formulated into doctrinal statements and to confirm that my thesis is not novel.

Though I am a Reformed Baptist subscribing to the Second London Confession of 1677/89, it is hoped that my thesis will help others in various ecclesiastical traditions. I assume that most (if not all) of my readers have either read Calvin's *Institutes*[1] on this subject or are aware of the Reformed view of the Supper as a means of grace as formulated, for example, by the Westminster Assembly. This means I am assuming some knowledge of the exegetical, theological, and historical issues involved with advocating the Supper as a means of grace. This also means that my work is aimed at pastors, theological students, and others who are able (and willing) to follow somewhat detailed exegetical and theological argumentation which results in doctrinal formulation.

As you work your way through the biblical section of the book (primarily chapters 3–5), you will notice that the words of the apostle Paul function as the predominant influence informing my thinking. Here is my justification for such influence. The

1. John Calvin, *Institutes of the Christian Religion* (Philadelphia: The Westminster Press, 1960), IV.viii-xviii.

apostle Paul is, by common consent, *the* theologian of the writers of the New Testament. Geerhardus Vos claimed that Paul's was 'the greatest constructive mind ever at work on the data of Christianity'.[2] Thomas D. Bernard calls Paul 'the great doctor of the Church'.[3] Bernard sees this distinction between the writings of the other apostles and Paul's:

> If the others were the Apostles of the manifestation of Christ, [Paul] was the Apostle of its *results;* and, in the fact of passing under *his* teaching, we have sufficient warning that we are advancing from the lessons which the life, and the character, and the words of Jesus gave, into the distinct exposition of the redemption, the reconciliation, the salvation which result from his appearing. In this way it was provided that the two correlative kinds of teaching, which the Church received at the first, should be left to the Church forever in the distinctness of their respective developments; for this distinctness of development in the second kind of teaching is both announced and secured by its being confided to St. Paul.[4]

Paul's writings bring Christian doctrine to its fullness and maturity. He was given the ability, like no other human author of Scripture, to apply the redemptive-historical accomplishments of Christ to the conditions and circumstances of first-century Christianity. Paul's epistles have a unique vocabulary. It is the vocabulary of the application of accomplished redemption. It is 'in Christ' theology brought to the contingencies Paul's converts faced. What Edward M. Blaiklock says of the entire corpus of the New Testament epistles applies in a unique way to Paul's:

---

2. Geerhardus Vos, *The Pauline Eschatology* (Phillipsburg, NJ: P&R Publishing, 1930, Reprinted 1991), 149.

3. Thomas Dehany Bernard, *The Progress of Doctrine in the New Testament* (New York: American Tract Society, n.d.), 155.

4. Bernard, *Progress of Doctrine*, 155.

> The letters of the NT form the corpus of Christianity's theology, its Christology, its evangel, the nature of the church, the state of man, the plan of salvation, the integration of the Testaments, and Christian eschatology.[5]

The Gospels contain the facts of redemption accomplished – the life, death, and resurrection of Christ (i.e., his sufferings and glory); the epistles, and especially Paul's, contain the implications, consequences, and applications of redemption accomplished. Paul is the greatest expounder of the Christian gospel of justification by faith alone and of the wonderfully glorious Christ-centered, resurrection-dependent eschatological hope. This hope is dependent upon Christ's resurrection as the first fruits of a great resurrection-harvest to come. The Holy Spirit is the pledge and down-payment that assures believers that what God did for the Messiah in his resurrection, he will do for all those in Jesus when he comes in glory. What God began to do in the life-history of every believer, he will complete when Jesus comes. It is in Paul's epistles that these glorious redemptive realities are expounded and Christianity comes to revelational-theological maturity.

There are three other reasons for concentrating upon Paul: he wrote about the nature of the Lord's Supper as communion (1 Cor. 10:16); he articulates a rich theology of the Spirit in relation to the redemptive benefits of Christ that come to elect sinners on earth (Eph. 1:3); and he ties that theology to the use of means (Eph. 3:14ff.).

Some may conclude that my work is actually an attempt at a Pauline view of the Supper as a means of grace (as if that were necessarily a bad thing). It is important to remind ourselves that

---

5. Edward M. Blaiklock, 'The Epistolary Literature' in Frank E. Gaebelein, Editor, *The Expositor's Bible Commentary, Volume I* (Grand Rapids: Zondervan Publishing House, 1979), 552.

Paul's writings, along with the other canonical books, are Holy Scripture and have the same divine author (2 Tim. 3:15-17; 2 Pet. 3:15-16). So in effect, what Paul says about the Supper (and upon any other subject) is what God says. The reader will also notice that the discussion focusing on Paul interprets him in the context of the entirety of Scripture. This is important because all doctrines of Scripture are, at various levels, inter-related and mutually dependent.

A word on Chapter 6 may be appropriate. It comprises a survey of some of the Reformed tradition's confessions and catechisms on the Supper as a means of grace. My purpose for this chapter is twofold – to show that my exegetical work and theological formulation are not novel and to help readers understand what the confessions and catechisms mean.

A final word on the Greek exegetical work contained in this book may help some. I included as much Greek as I thought necessary for the goal of this work and its intended audience. There are times when I transliterate and other times I include an English translation (most times the NASB and sometimes my own). Anyone with two years of Greek should be able to follow the discussion and some with little or no Greek may be able to as well. I included what I did for the purpose of showing my work and helping readers see the process I took in order to get to the conclusions to which I have come. The reader will notice that understanding Paul often involves difficult syntactical questions. I have tried to face those questions head-on and explain why I take the views that I do. The reader will also notice that my views on thorny syntactical issues are not novel, idiosyncratic, or exclusively held by confessional Reformed commentators.

I am grateful to several friends who read various editions of this work along its way to completion. Most of them are faithful pastors of relatively unknown churches. When all the dust is clear on the last day, men like this from all ages of the church will see their mostly unseen and unknown work redound to the praise of the Lamb. This book is dedicated to these men and many others like them.

Introduction

The subject matter of this book is vitally important for confessional Reformed churches[1] and all other local churches. I am convinced from the word of God that the Lord's Supper is a vital part of local church life because it was ordained by the Lord Jesus to be a means of grace and more than a memory. I hope you will agree with me once I am finished.

At the outset of our discussion, it may be helpful to get the theology of the Lord's Supper I will be arguing for in our minds. It is my conviction that the doctrinal formulation of the Lord's Supper in the Second London Confession of 1677/89 (2nd LCF)

1. By 'confessional Reformed churches' I intend those local churches that subscribe to one of the Reformation/post-Reformation Reformed symbolic documents – The Three Forms of Unity (the Belgic Confession, the Canons of Dort, and the Heidelberg Catechism) and the various documents related to the work of the Westminster Assembly (its confession and catechisms, the Savoy Declaration, and the Second London Confession of 1677/89). The last named document is an English Particular Baptist product. It will be argued that the English Particular Baptists of that day stood in substantial continuity with other Reformed theologians on the issue of the Lord's Supper as a means of grace. If the reader has scruples about Baptists claiming to be Reformed, simply substitute the word 'Covenantal' or 'Confessional' or 'Particular' for 'Reformed'. My point is more theological than historical.

accurately reflects the complex[2] teaching of Scripture on this important issue. The 2nd LCF stands in substantial theological continuity with the Westminster Confession of Faith (WCF) and other Reformation and post-Reformation creedal statements on this and many other issues. Here are two paragraphs from the 2nd LCF on the Lord's Supper that capture the theology of the Lord's Supper advocated in this book.

> The supper of the Lord Jesus was instituted by Him the same night wherein He was betrayed, to be observed in His churches, unto the end of the world, for the perpetual remembrance, and shewing forth the sacrifice of Himself in His death, *confirmation of the faith of believers in all the benefits thereof, their spiritual nourishment,* and *growth in Him,* their further engagement in, and to all duties which they owe to Him; and *to be a bond and pledge of their communion with Him,* and with each other. (30:1; emphases added)[3]

> Worthy receivers, outwardly partaking of the visible elements in this ordinance, do then also *inwardly by faith, really and indeed, yet not carnally and corporally, but spiritually receive, and feed upon Christ crucified, and all the benefits of His death;* the body and blood of Christ being then not corporally or carnally, *but spiritually present to the faith of believers* in that ordinance, as the elements themselves are to their outward senses. (30:7; emphases added)

If you read the sections of the confession quoted above, you can see why the sub-title of this book is 'More than a Memory'. Though there is a memorial aspect to the Lord's Supper, it is more than that. I hope to show you what that means in the pages that follow.

---

2. By 'complex' I do not mean difficult or obscure. I mean multi-faceted.
3. All quotations of the 2nd LCF come from *The Baptist Confession of Faith & The Baptist Catechism* (Vestavia Hills, AL: Solid Ground Christian Books and Carlisle, PA: Reformed Baptist Publications, 2010).

A few words about the title

I have entitled this book *The Lord's Supper as a Means of Grace: More than a Memory*. The title seeks to encapsulate both *positive instruction* and *needed correction*.

The positive instruction comes in the first part of the title: *The Lord's Supper as a Means of Grace*. The 2nd LCF asserts that the Lord's Supper confirms the faith of believers in the benefits of Christ's death, that it nourishes their souls, that it causes growth in Christ, that it is a bond and pledge of believers' communion with Christ, that worthy receivers spiritually receive and feed upon Christ crucified and all the benefits of his death by faith, and that Christ is spiritually present at the Supper. This is the language of means of grace. My primary goal in this book is to concentrate on *how* the Lord's Supper is spiritually nourishing to the souls of believers, how it effects or produces spiritual growth in worthy partakers, or how it is a means of grace. But what are 'means of grace'?

I define means of grace as the delivery systems God has instituted to bring grace – that is, spiritual power, spiritual change, spiritual help, spiritual fortitude, spiritual blessings – to needy souls on the earth. Grace comes from our Father, through the Son, by the Spirit ordinarily in conjunction with the ordained means. The means of grace are those conduits through which Christ alters, modifies, adjusts, changes, transforms, and develops souls on the earth. Herman Bavinck says, 'Christ is and remains the acquisitor as well as the distributor of grace.'[4] That is, Christ acquired grace *for* us and distributes grace *to* or *in* us. In order to get acquired grace *to* or *in* us, God has ordained means through which it is distributed. The means of grace, then, are God's delivery systems through which that which was acquired *for* us

4. Herman Bavinck, *Reformed Dogmatics: Holy Spirit, Church, and New Creation*, IV, translated by John Vriend (Grand Rapids: Baker Academic, 2008), 448.

gets distributed or delivered *to* or *in* us. I will be working with the assumption that the Word of God, prayer, and the church sacraments or ordinances[5] of baptism and the Lord's Supper are the primary or ordinary means through which grace from heaven comes to souls on the earth.[6]

It will be argued that the Bible teaches that one of the means instituted by Christ to bring grace from heaven to elect and gospel-believing souls on the earth is the Lord's Supper. The Lord's

5. I use the terms 'sacrament' and 'ordinance' interchangeably. Though the 2nd LCF uses the term 'ordinance,' English Particular Baptists in the seventeenth century also used the term 'sacrament' to refer to both baptism and the Lord's Supper (Cf. *An Orthodox Catechism*, Hercules Collins, 'Of the Sacraments,' where the terms are used interchangeably. Collins was a signatory of the 2nd LCF. His catechism was first published in 1680. It can be found in James M. Renihan, Editor, *True Confessions: Baptist Documents in the Reformed Family* (Owensboro, KY: RBAP, 2004), 254ff. See also William Kiffin, *A Sober Discourse of Right to Church-Communion* (London: Geo. Larkin, 1681), 23 [I will quote this work in the last chapter.]). Kiffin was a leading English Particular Baptist and also a signatory of the 2nd LCF. It seems that 'ordinance' refers to dominical origin – ordained (by the Lord Christ) – and 'sacrament' refers to function – a sign and means of grace (Cf. Richard A. Muller, *Dictionary of Latin and Greek Theological Terms* [Grand Rapids: Baker Book House, 1985, Second printing, September 1986], 267-68 under the entry 'sacramentum' for a discussion of the Protestant Scholastic use of this term 'sacrament'). Steve Weaver's unpublished, *Christ Spiritually Present and Believers Spiritually Nourished: The Lord's Supper in Seventeenth-Century Particular Baptist Life* has ample primary source documentation of further proof that the seventeenth-century English Particular Baptists used 'sacrament' and 'ordinance' interchangeably. The reason for using 'ordinance' in the 2nd LCF was not to deny the concept of 'sacrament' but probably to stress dominical institution (Cf. Michael A. G. Haykin, *Kiffin, Knollys and Keach: Rediscovering our English Baptist heritage* [Leeds, England: Reformation Today Trust, 1996], 78 and James M. Renihan, *Edification and Beauty: The Practical Ecclesiology of the English Particular Baptists, 1675-1705* [Eugene, OR: Wipf & Stock Publishers, 2008], 143, n.119). For eighteenth-century evidence that English Particular Baptists continued to use 'sacrament' and 'ordinance' interchangeably, see Benjamin Beddome, *A Scriptural Exposition of the Baptist Catechism* (Birmingham, AL: Solid Ground Christian Books, 2006), 156-57. It is of interest to note that the WCF uses the term 'sacrament' in chapters XIV and XXVII-XXIX in various places and also uses the word 'ordinance' to refer to baptism (XXVIII.5-6) and the Lord's Supper (XXIX.3).

6. This is the view of the 2nd LCF, 14:1 and the WCF, XIV.1. For a helpful recent discussion on the means of grace as 'God's Media,' see Daniel R. Hyde, *In Living Color: Images of Christ and the Means of Grace* (Grandville, MI: Reformed Fellowship, Inc., 2009), 89-160.

Supper is a soul-changing, soul-altering, spiritually nurturing ordinance as blessed by the Spirit of God to that end.

The needed correction mentioned above comes in the second part of the title: *More than a Memory*. If you are like me, you have probably been taught that the Lord's Supper is a memorial meal, instituted by Christ to function as a periodic reminder of his death on behalf of sinners. When churches partake of the Supper they are doing something together – remembering Christ's death. In this sense, communion is horizontal. *We* are sharing in the memory of a redemptive-historical fact of the past, *we* are remembering the fact that Christ died for us. But is the Lord's Supper only backward-looking, only retrospective? Is it only a memorial of a past event? Or is it more than a memory? Is it primarily something *we* do or is it something through which *God* acts? I will attempt to prove to you in the pages that follow that the Lord's Supper is more than a memory (though it is certainly that). If you are like me, this may be a needed correction in your thinking and practice.

The difficulty of this subject

This subject is a difficult one to consider and work through for at least three reasons. *First*, it is difficult because of the amount of ink spilled over this issue at the time of the Reformation. Part of the reason it is difficult is surely due to the various positions coming out of the Reformation period and the complexity of those historical-theological debates.[7] More ink was spilled over the issue

7. For Reformed discussions on the Reformation debates concerning the Lord's Supper, see Bavinck, *Reformed Dogmatics*, IV:556-61; Michael Horton, *The Christian Faith: A Systematic Theology for Pilgrim's on the Way* (Grand Rapids: Zondervan, 2011), 803-23; Timothy George, *Theology of the Reformers* (Nashville, TN: Broadman Press, 1988), 144-58; Robert Letham, *The Lord's Supper: Eternal Word in Broken Bread* (Phillipsburg, NJ: P&R Publishing, 2001), 19-29; Malcolm Maclean, *The Lord's Supper* (Fearn, Ross-shire, Scotland: Christian Focus Publication, Mentor Imprint, 2009), 43-68; Keith A. Mathison, *Given For You: Reclaiming Calvin's Doctrine of the*

of the sacrament of communion or the Lord's Supper at the time of the Reformation than over the issue of justification *sola fide*.[8]

The Lord's Supper is vitally important for the church (or at least it ought to be and it certainly used to be). It has been and continues to be fertile ground for disagreement among good men. I think it was when Luther finally concluded he could not agree with Zwingli on this issue that he said, 'Zwingli is of another spirit.' The Reformation debates on this issue, then, lead me to conclude that this is a difficult subject.

A *second* reason why this is a difficult subject is because of the diverse views among Christians in our own day. Some view the Supper as only a memorial. Others view it as a means of grace, highlighting the presence of Christ and the ministry of the Spirit who serves grace to the souls of believers. Lutherans hold that Christ's human nature is somehow present with the elements of wine and bread. Sorting through the various views can be perplexing, adding to the difficulty of this subject.

A *third* reason why this is a difficult subject is because of the tendency in everyone to allow wrong presuppositions to cloud judgment. Everyone brings preconceived notions into discussions which often shield us from understanding what someone else is arguing. I have found this to be the case with reference to the Lord's Supper in my own pilgrimage. I was raised Roman Catholic and converted to Christ through the ministry of a non-denominational, evangelical church. Both of these experiences tainted my mind in terms of what the Lord's Supper is and ought to be. My experience prejudiced me against certain aspects of the historical discussion concerning the Lord's Supper as a means of grace and more than a

---

Lord's Supper (Phillipsburg, NJ: P&R Publishing, 2002), 239-68; and Jon D. Payne, *John Owen on the Lord's Supper* (Edinburgh, Scotland and Carlisle, PA: The Banner of Truth Trust, 2004), 18-50.

8. Mathison, *Given for You*, xv.

memory. This made it difficult for me to understand, for instance, what Calvin means on this issue (not that I necessarily agree with or even understand all that he says). In my own experience, I have found that I did not believe or, in some cases, understand what others were saying because I had already made up my mind. But, sadly, this was not because I had adequately studied the issue and listened humbly to the discussion of the great minds of the church. Though it is impossible to do presuppositionless study on any level, we need to make sure that we come to this (and every) issue with the proper working assumptions.

These are three reasons I think the subject under consideration puts me at the bottom of a hill that seems at times insurmountable. If great minds can't agree on this issue, who am I to think I can clear up the fog? With various views held by good and godly people, can we really come to a definitive conclusion? How can the reader be sure the writer's presuppositions are right? As will become obvious, I am not advocating anything new. The view of the Lord's Supper as a means of grace I am arguing for is not novel. It has many advocates – Baptists and Paedobaptists, both past and present. My consolation is in this fact: when the Lord's word is opened and explained accurately he makes things men have made obscure to be clear.

The difficulties involved with this subject should not stop us from taking a position. We can and must take a position on whether or not the Lord's Supper is a means of grace and more than a memory, even though it may be difficult to come by. Either it is a means of grace and more than a memory or it is not. But once we take a position, we must both be knowledgeable of what we believe and gracious toward those who might differ with us. Though this is an important issue, the possession of eternal life does not depend upon taking one view of the Lord's Supper or another.

The specific focus of this study

The specific focus of this study is *not* primarily to prove to you that the Lord's Supper is a means of grace, though I hope to do that. The title of this book assumes that the Lord's Supper is a means of grace. I am a confessional Reformed Baptist and both the confessional and catechetical documents of Reformed Baptists *explicitly affirm* the Lord's Supper as a means of grace.[9]

My specific focus is to show you *how* the Lord's Supper is a means of grace. My answer is that the Lord's Supper is a means of grace because of what the Holy Spirit does in the souls of believers when local churches partake of it. The Spirit effects or enhances present communion between the exalted Redeemer and his pilgrim people on the earth. Or it can be stated this way: the Lord's Supper is a means of grace through which Christ is present by his divine nature and through which the Holy Spirit nourishes the souls of believers with the benefits wrought for us in Christ's human nature which is now glorified and in heaven at the right hand of the Father.

The method of this study

I have struggled with how to present this material. Should I give the historical-theological-confessional position first or what I see as the Bible's teaching? Or should I give the biblical arguments showing that and how the Lord's Supper is a means of grace and then move to the confessional formulation of the doctrine? This question of method is no small issue. As you will notice below, we will study the Bible and the symbolic documents of the Reformed tradition, and in that order.[10] The Bible alone is

9. See Chapter 6 below.

10. This does not necessarily infer that reversing the order is a faulty method. The important thing is to allow the Bible its place as the only infallible source of authority for Christian doctrine and to allow ourselves to be taught by others, many of whom have gone before us.

our infallible source of authority on the Lord's Supper. However, the Bible has been studied by faithful believers for over 2,000 years. Its primary doctrines have been formulated into creedal statements. These creedal statements reflect the best corporate thinking on the Bible and its teachings. Consulting the mind of the church over the centuries as embodied in its creedal statements is a safe guide to insure we are not inventing new doctrines, nor imposing idiosyncratic nuances upon the Bible, nor reading the Bible anachronistically – importing contemporary forms of thought upon the ancient text and reading it through those lenses. As a student of the Bible, I use various sources to help me understand the text. When I go to the Bible with a question and begin to answer that question, I consult the Bible itself, lexicons, commentaries, articles, books, systematic theologies, sermons, and the creeds, confessions, and catechisms of the Christian church throughout the ages. These study-helps guide me in the conversation that has been and is taking place concerning what the Bible teaches. Studying the Bible along with competent teachers is a safe guide. It keeps us where the Spirit of God has been helping the church of God understand the word of God.

I have decided to present *some* of the biblical evidence concerning the nature of the Lord's Supper as a means of grace and then show you *where* and *how* the confessional and catechetical data reflects this teaching of the Bible. Our study will be pursued under the following four headings: first, 'The Terminology connected to the Lord's Supper in the New Testament' (Chapter 1); second, 'The Biblical Data which Advocate the Lord's Supper as a Means of Grace (Chapters 2-4); third, 'The Confessional and Catechetical Formulation of the Lord's Supper as a Means of Grace in the Reformed Creedal Tradition' (Chapter 5); and fourth, 'Final Thoughts' (Chapter 6).

1

The Terminology connected to the Lord's Supper in the New Testament

The New Testament uses various words and phrases to describe the Lord's Supper. No one term or phrase expresses all of the various dimensions of its meaning. Each description contributes to its overall meaning in a unique way. In this brief chapter, we will survey the New Testament terminology to lay a foundation for subsequent discussion.[1]

The New Testament on the Lord's Supper

The giving of thanks

The Lord's Supper involves the giving of thanks (Matt. 26:26-29; Mark 14:22-24; and 1 Cor. 11:23-26).

> [26]While they were eating, Jesus took *some* bread, and after a blessing, He broke *it* and gave *it* to the disciples, and said, 'Take, eat; this is My body.' [27]And when He had taken a cup and given

1. This survey is not exhaustive. For similar surveys, see Letham, *The Lord's Supper*, 3-18; Maclean, *The Lord's Supper*, 13-39; Mathison, *Given For You*, 203-35; and Richard D. Phillips, *What is the Lord's Supper?* (Phillipsburg, NJ: P&R Publishing, 2005), 7-13.

thanks, He gave *it* to them, saying, 'Drink from it, all of you; [28]for this is My blood of the covenant, which is poured out for many for forgiveness of sins. [29]'But I say to you, I will not drink of this fruit of the vine from now on until that day when I drink it new with you in My Father's kingdom.' (Matt. 26:26-29)

[22]While they were eating, He took *some* bread, and after a blessing He broke *it*, and gave *it* to them, and said, 'Take *it*; this is My body.' [23]And when He had taken a cup *and* given thanks, He gave *it* to them, and they all drank from it. [24]And He said to them, 'This is My blood of the covenant, which is poured out for many.' (Mark 14:22-24)

[23]For I received from the Lord that which I also delivered to you, that the Lord Jesus in the night in which He was betrayed took bread; [24]and when He had given thanks, He broke it and said, 'This is My body, which is for you; do this in remembrance of Me.' [25]In the same way *He took* the cup also after supper, saying, 'This cup is the new covenant in My blood; do this, as often as you drink *it*, in remembrance of Me.' [26]For as often as you eat this bread and drink the cup, you proclaim the Lord's death until He comes. (1 Cor. 11:23-26)

Because the Lord's Supper involves the giving of thanks the early, post-apostolic church identified it as the Eucharist, coming from the Greek word for thanksgiving.[2] At the Lord's Supper we are to express our thankfulness for the giving up of the Son of God for the eternal well-being of our souls and bodies. This is normally done in a formal way by the presiding minister thanking the Lord,

---

2. Cf. *The Didache* 9:1-5, esp. 9:1 and 5 (where the term 'Eucharist' [from the Gk. εὐχαριστία] clearly refers to the Lord's Supper) in Michael W. Holmes, Editor and Translator, *The Apostolic Fathers: Greek Texts and English Translations*, third edition (Grand Rapids: Baker Academic, 2007), 357-59. *The Didache* ('The Teaching') is an early church teaching manual. It was compiled most likely over several decades (possibly beginning in the first century) and completed sometime in the mid- to late-second century.

which also functions as a prayer of consecration.[3] Without Christ giving himself up as he did, there is no hope for sinners. When we take the Lord's Supper, we are to express our thankfulness, our gratitude. This concept of thankfulness is probably one of the reasons we often say, 'We are going to *celebrate* the Lord's Supper.' Thankfulness is very appropriate, even necessary, when churches come together to take the Lord's Supper.

The breaking of bread

The Lord's Supper is called 'the breaking of bread' (Acts 2:42 and 20:7). Acts 2:42 says, 'They [the disciples] were continually devoting themselves to the apostles' teaching and to fellowship, to the breaking of bread and to prayer.' Acts 20:7 says, 'On the first day of the week, when we were gathered together to break bread, Paul *began* talking to them, intending to leave the next day, and he prolonged his message until midnight.' Both of these references likely refer to the Lord's Supper. In Acts 27:35 (notice the context beginning in v. 33) breaking of bread and giving thanks refers to eating food or a common meal. The breaking of bread in Acts 2:42 and 20:7, however, refers to the words of institution given initially by our Lord Christ and passed on to the first churches by the apostles (cf. 1 Cor. 11:23). Breaking bread 'is a graphic portrayal of [Christ's] death on the cross, where his body was broken to secure our redemption.'[4] When we break bread as churches, we have a graphic portrayal of Christ's death for us.

Sharing in the blood and body of Christ

The Lord's Supper is called 'sharing in the blood of Christ' and 'in the body of Christ' (1 Cor. 10:16).[5] 'Is not the cup of blessing which we bless a sharing in the blood of Christ? Is not the bread

3. We will discuss the importance of prayer during the Lord's Supper subsequently.

4. Letham, *The Lord's Supper*, 5.

5. We will discuss the translation of 1 Cor. 10:16 in Chapter 3.

which we break a sharing in the body of Christ?' The KJV translates 'sharing' as 'communion' which is why we sometimes call the Lord's Supper 'Communion.' Notice that this 'sharing' or 'communion' (KJV, NKJV, ASV [1901]) is a present-tense reality. It is something that takes place through the Lord's Supper. I will argue later from this that the Lord's Supper is more than a memorial meal. It does not call us to look only to the past – 'Do this in remembrance of Me.' There is something about the Supper that involves a present reality, a 'sharing' or 'communion' with Christ and the benefits he brings to our souls. We will discuss this in more detail in chapter two.

The cup and table of the Lord

The Lord's Supper is called 'the cup' and 'table of the Lord' (1 Cor. 10:21). 'You cannot drink the cup of the Lord and the cup of demons; you cannot partake of the table of the Lord and the table of demons.' This rite belongs to Christ the Lord. He instituted it. The table at which it occurs is his. The cup is his, as well. He presides over this table. He is Lord of the cup. He is not a distant, though interested, on-looker.

The Lord's Supper

The Lord's Supper is the Lord's (1 Cor. 11:20). 'Therefore when you meet together, it is not to eat the Lord's Supper.' The Lord's Supper is his. He owns it. It belongs to him. He presides over it. The food served is his. It is no ordinary meal. It is uniquely connected to his lordship. This is the only time in the Bible it is called *the Lord's Supper*. Notice that it is called the *Lord's* Supper. This word translated 'Lord's' (κυριακός [*kuriakos*]) is used twice in the New Testament – 1 Corinthians 11:20 and Revelation 1:10. It is an adjective. In 1 Corinthians 11:20 it modifies the noun 'Supper' and in Revelation 1:10 it modifies the noun 'day'. It means 'belonging to the Lord'.[6] It is called the Lord's Supper after his resurrection and ascension. The same goes for the *Lord's* Day (Rev. 1:10). The Lord's Day is a day peculiarly belonging to the resurrected and ascended Lord Jesus. The Supper is the same. It is a Supper that peculiarly belongs to him as resurrected and ascended. Though all suppers come from the Lord, not all suppers are 'the *Lord's*' in this sense. And, though all days come from the Lord, not all days are 'the *Lord's*.' There is both a distinction of suppers and a distinction of days in the New Testament. Just as the Lord's Supper has peculiar religious significance for Christians, so does the Lord's Day. All suppers are not alike, neither are all days alike. Both the Lord's Supper and the Lord's Day are Jesus Christ's in a unique manner and both get their names after he rises from the dead and ascends into heaven.

Some practical observations

The Lord's Supper: covenantal meal

The Lord's Supper is a covenantal meal (Matt. 26:26-29 and Mark 14:22-24). As the Old Covenant had a covenantal meal connected to covenantal blood in the special presence of God, so does the New Covenant. Listen to Exodus 24:1-11:

> Then He said to Moses, 'Come up to the LORD, you and Aaron, Nadab and Abihu and seventy of the elders of Israel, and you shall worship at a distance. [2]'Moses alone, however, shall come

6. For further discussion of this word, see H. Bietenhard, 'Lord' in, Colin Brown, Editor, *The New International Dictionary of New Testament Theology*, (Grand Rapids: Zondervan Publishing House, 1986), 2:518 referenced as NIDNTT hereafter and Richard C. Barcellos, 'The New Testament Theology of the Sabbath: Christ, the Change of the Day and the Name of the Day' in *Reformed Baptist Theological Review* V:1 (Spring 2008), 58-63. There I deal briefly with translational issues and the grammatical and theological relationship between 1 Cor. 11:20 and Rev. 1:10.

> near to the LORD, but they shall not come near, nor shall the people come up with him.' [3]Then Moses came and recounted to the people all the words of the LORD and all the ordinances; and all the people answered with one voice and said, 'All the words which the LORD has spoken we will do!' [4]Moses wrote down all the words of the LORD. Then he arose early in the morning, and built an altar at the foot of the mountain with twelve pillars for the twelve tribes of Israel. [5]He sent young men of the sons of Israel, and they offered burnt offerings and sacrificed young bulls as peace offerings to the LORD. [6]Moses took half of the blood and put *it* in basins, and the *other* half of the blood he sprinkled on the altar. [7]Then he took the book of the covenant and read *it* in the hearing of the people; and they said, 'All that the LORD has spoken we will do, and we will be obedient!' [8]So Moses took the blood and sprinkled *it* on the people, and said, 'Behold the blood of the covenant, which the LORD has made with you in accordance with all these words.' [9]Then Moses went up with Aaron, Nadab and Abihu, and seventy of the elders of Israel, [10]and they saw the God of Israel; and under His feet there appeared to be a pavement of sapphire, as clear as the sky itself. [11]Yet He did not stretch out His hand against the nobles of the sons of Israel; and they saw God, and they ate and drank.

The 'blood of the covenant' indicates entrance into covenantal relations with God. Thus, when we take the Lord's Supper, it is a covenantal renewal meal. It does not bring us into covenant with God; it reminds us that we are in covenant with him through Christ and enhances that covenantal bond. That's why the Confession says, 'The Supper is ... [for the] further engagement in, and to all the duties which [believers] owe to Him; and to be a bond and pledge of [believers'] communion with Him, and with each other' (2nd LCF 30:1; WCF XXIX.1). When we take the Supper we are reasserting allegiance to the exalted Christ together. Michael Horton says:

> The Lord's Supper, then, is a covenant meal. That means that while it is first of all a ratification of God's pledge to us, it also ratifies our pledge to God and to each other. It has both vertical and horizontal dimensions.[7]

The Lord's Supper: memorial ordinance

The Lord's Supper calls us to look back; it is connected to the past – 'Do this in remembrance of Me' (1 Cor. 11:24). It has a memorial element to it, just like the Passover of the Old Testament (Exod. 12; 34:25; Lev. 9; Deut. 16). It is retrospective. It has something to do with the past. It looks back to redemption accomplished. The death of Christ, which was the exhaustion of damnation for us, is its memorial terminus, its stopping point, its target. When we take the Lord's Supper, let us never forget what we are remembering: the just One dying for unjust ones that he might bring us into the safe presence of God (1 Pet. 3:18). The Lord's Supper reminds us that redemption has been won for us by Christ, the captain of our salvation who brings many sons to glory (Heb. 2:10).

The Lord's Supper: present communion

The Lord's Supper has a present, spiritual benefit to it. 'Is not the cup of blessing which we bless a sharing in the blood of Christ? Is not the bread which we break a sharing in the body of Christ?' (1 Cor. 10:16). We commune together in or share together the present benefits of his blood and his body given for us long ago. It is a covenantal meal. It is a bond and pledge of present communion with Christ and the benefits he purchased *for* us and gives *to* us.

The Lord's Supper: eschatological anticipation

The Lord's Supper is connected to the future (Matt. 26:29 and 1 Cor. 11:26). In Matthew 26:29, Jesus said, 'But I say to you,

---

7. Michael Horton, *God of Promise: Introducing Covenant Theology* (Grand Rapids: Baker Books, 2006), 159.

I will not drink of this fruit of the vine from now on until that day when I drink it new with you in My Father's kingdom.' In 1 Corinthians 11:26, Paul said, 'For as often as you eat this bread and drink the cup, you proclaim the Lord's death until He comes.' Listen to Geerhardus Vos commenting on 1 Corinthians 11:26:

> When Paul enjoins his readers to proclaim the Lord's death 'until he shall come,' this certainly is not intended as a mere chronological remark concerning the perpetual validity of the observance of the Supper in the church. It suggests rather the idea that when the Lord shall have come the necessity for further observance of the sacrament will no longer exist, and this in turn gives rise to the thought that in the present observance of it there is an anticipation of what the eschatological state has in store for the believer.[8]

The Lord's Supper is anticipatory. It not only points to the past and ministers grace in the present, it also points to the future, when the Son of God will drink of the fruit of the vine with us.

The Lord's Supper: three tenses (past, present, future)

There are three tenses of the Lord's Supper – past (the accomplishment of redemption), present (the application of redemption), and future (the consummation of redemption). When we take the Supper, we do so in remembrance of Christ's death. At the Supper, we enjoy present communion with Christ. But our Lord said he will drink with his people in the future in his Father's kingdom. It is of interest to note that at the inauguration of the Old (Exod. 24:1-11) and New Covenants (Matt. 26:26-29) God was with his people, and eating occurred. There is also a prospect held out for us, an eschatological feast in the New Heavens and

---

8. Geerhardus Vos in Danny E. Olinger, Editor, *A Geerhardus Vos Anthology: Biblical and Theological Insights Alphabetically Arranged* (Phillipsburg, NJ: P&R Publishing, 2005), 185.

the New Earth (Matt. 26:29; Luke 14:15; Rev. 19:9). There will be eating and feasting at the consummation. All of this is due to the blood of the Lamb, slain for sinners, in order to bring us to God. The Lord's Supper reminds us of the past, blesses us in the present, and looks to future eating, future feasting with the Lamb in all his glory. As Vos said, in it 'there is an anticipation of what the eschatological state has in store for the believer'.[9]

9. Vos in Olinger, *Anthology*, 185.

2

Communion at the Lord's Supper

The next three chapters discuss the biblical data which advocate the Lord's Supper as a means of grace. They will focus on two of Paul's letters – 1 Corinthians and Ephesians. My reason for concentrating on Paul was presented in the Preface. In short, Paul is the theologian of the application of redemption. He deals explicitly with the Lord's Supper as a means of grace and provides theological rationale for how communion with Christ occurs through it.

My purpose in writing does not permit me to do justice to all the biblical data on the issue of the Lord's Supper as a means of grace. Many others have sought to do that and are worth consulting for a more comprehensive approach.[1] I have chosen to limit this section to two types of texts. These texts indicate the nature of the Lord's Supper as a means of grace and explain

1. Bavinck, *Reformed Dogmatics*, IV:540-85; Louis Berkhof, *Systematic Theology* (Grand Rapids: William B. Eerdmans Publishing Company, 1939, Reprinted 1986), 644-58; Calvin, *Institutes*, IV.viii-xviii; Horton, *The Christian Faith*, 798-827; Letham, *The Lord's Supper*; Maclean, *The Lord's Supper*; and Mathison, *Given For You*.

how grace gets from heaven to earth. First of all, we will look at the most important text in Paul which speaks about the *nature* of the Lord's Supper (1 Cor. 10:16). Then we will look at two texts which address the ministry of the Holy Spirit in relation to our exalted Redeemer in bringing mediatorial, redemptive benefits to the souls of believers on the earth (Eph. 1:3 and 3:16-17).

1 Corinthians 10:16

> Is not the cup of blessing which we bless a sharing in the blood of Christ? Is not the bread which we break a sharing in the body of Christ?

This may be the most important text on the *nature* of the Lord's Supper as means of grace in the New Testament (certainly in Paul's letters). Notice that Paul asks two questions both related to the Lord's Supper. The answer to both questions is a resounding yes. The cup of blessing *is* a sharing in the blood of Christ and the bread which we break *is* a sharing in the body of Christ. But what does this mean and why does Paul bring this up in this passage which deals with idolatry (1 Cor. 10:14)? To understand its teaching properly, we must first get acquainted with its context.

In 1 Corinthians 8:1, Paul begins dealing with 'things sacrificed to idols' (8:1) and, more specifically, 'eating of things sacrificed to idols' (8:4). This section ends at 11:1. David E. Garland helps us understand what Paul is doing.

> Paul's lengthy discussion of idol food (8:1-11:1) is grounded in his christological monotheism, which defines the people of God over against those who worship many so-called gods and lords in their sundry guise. As a cosmopolitan city, Corinth was a religious melting pot, with older and newer religions flourishing side-by-side. Most persons could accommodate

> all gods and goddesses into their religious behavior, and they could choose from a great cafeteria line of religious practices. The Christian confession of one God and one Lord, however, requires exclusive loyalty to God as Father and to Christ as Lord (8:6).[2]

Paul is arguing against the Christian's participation in the religious syncretism so common in Corinth (and ancient Greece and Rome). In the process of doing this, several practical matters come to the surface, which we will see below.

In 1 Corinthians 10:1-13 Paul refers to ancient Israel as an example of privileged people abusing privileges (10:1-5) and committing idolatry (10:7). In light of this, he exhorts the Corinthians to learn from their bad example and 'not crave evil things' (10:6), to avoid idolatry (10:7), immorality (10:8), trying the Lord (10:9), and grumbling (10:10). He admonishes them to learn from ancient Israel (10:11), take heed (10:12), and be reminded of the faithfulness of God in the midst of temptations (10:13).

In 1 Corinthians 10:23-33 Paul deals with eating meat 'sold in the market' (1 Cor. 10:25). Though they are free to eat such meat (10:25-27), there are times it is best not to for 'conscience' sake' (10:28). Whatever they do, they are to make sure it is not seeking their own good (10:24) and is done for the glory of God (10:31), giving no offense to Jews, Greeks, or the church of God (10:32). It is important to note that this section deals with an indifferent matter and not idolatry, a violation of the law of God. Paul's discussion envisions various scenarios in which Corinthian believers might have found themselves. Roy E. Ciampa and Brian S. Rosner make this helpful observation:

---

2. David E. Garland, '1 Corinthians, Book of' in Kevin J. Vanhoozer, General Editor, *Dictionary for Theological Interpretation of the Bible* (Grand Rapids: Baker Academic, 2005), 136.

> Paul discusses a variety of contexts in which food might be eaten (as part of a pagan religious meal [10:14ff.], food purchased in the market for eating at home [10:25-26], food that one is offered when eating as a guest in another's home [10:27-30]) and gives advice for each context.[3]

The section in between 10:1-13 and 10:23-33 deals with idolatry. 'Therefore, my beloved, flee from idolatry' (10:14). This is no indifferent matter. Having mentioned the fact of the idolatry of some in ancient Israel (10:7), he now deals with contemporary idolatry in the context of church members at Corinth. Here is the text of 1 Corinthians 10:14-22 in full:

> [14]'Therefore, my beloved, flee from idolatry. [15]I speak as to wise men; you judge what I say. [16]Is not the cup of blessing which we bless a sharing in the blood of Christ? Is not the bread which we break a sharing in the body of Christ? [17]Since there is one bread, we who are many are one body; for we all partake of the one bread. [18]Look at the nation Israel; are not those who eat the sacrifices sharers in the altar? [19]What do I mean then? That a thing sacrificed to idols is anything, or that an idol is anything? [20]*No*, but *I say* that the things which the Gentiles sacrifice, they sacrifice to demons and not to God; and I do not want you to become sharers in demons. [21]You cannot drink the cup of the Lord and the cup of demons; you cannot partake of the table of the Lord and the table of demons. [22]Or do we provoke the Lord to jealousy? We are not stronger than He, are we?

This passage brings up many questions. We will answer some of them below. This much seems clear so far. In 1 Corinthians Paul deals with several church problems, one of them being idolatry (10:14). Apparently, some Corinthians thought 'they were free to

3. Roy E. Ciampa and Brian S. Rosner, '1 Corinthians' in G. K. Beale and D. A. Carson, Editors, *Commentary on the New Testament Use of the Old Testament* (Grand Rapids: Baker Academic, 2007), 729, referenced as CNTUOT hereafter.

continue participating in pagan sacrificial meals.'[4] Paul, however, strongly disagreed with them (10:14, '... flee from idolatry'). He is combating the sin of idolatry committed by some of the Corinthians by their 'participating in pagan religious meals.'[5]

The nature of the Lord's Supper: *koinonia*

Paul ends up shedding light on the *nature* of the Lord's Supper in 1 Corinthians 10:16. He does so as proof that participating in pagan sacrificial meals (1 Cor. 10:20-21) is a form of idolatry and must be avoided (1 Cor. 10:14). The important word here for our purposes is translated 'sharing' by the NASB. The Greek word is κοινωνία (*koinonia*), a feminine noun.[6] Also important are its qualifying phrases 'in the blood of Christ' (τοῦ αἵματος τοῦ Χριστοῦ) and 'in the body of Christ' (τοῦ σώματος τοῦ Χριστοῦ). What does *koinonia* – 'sharing' (NASB), 'participation' (ESV and NIV), or 'communion' (KJV, NKJV, and ASV [1901]) – mean? And what does *koinonia* 'in the blood of Christ' and 'in the body of Christ' mean?[7] So there are two questions we need to answer before proceeding. What does *koinonia* mean in this text? And how should we understand its modifying phrases 'in the blood of Christ' and 'in the body of Christ'?

There are various translational options for *koinonia* as noted above. The NASB translates it as 'a sharing'. The ESV and NIV translate it 'a participation'. The KJV and NKJV translate it 'the communion'. The ASV (1901) translates it 'a communion'. The ASV (1901), NASB, ESV, and NIV add the English indefinite 'a' and the

---

4. Mathison, *Given For You*, 227.

5. Ciampa and Rosner, CNTUOT, 728.

6. This becomes important in the discussion below.

7. The preposition 'in' is translated 'of' in the KJV, NKJV, and ASV (1901). We will explore the translational options below.

KJV and NKJV add 'the.'[8] Either way, I do not think the meaning is affected. The Greek-English lexicon abbreviated BDAG gives various entries under *koinonia* – close association involving mutual interests, sharing, association, communion, fellowship, close relationship, and participation.[9] We should not allow the various lexical options to frustrate us. Lexicons are not commentaries and often do not define words based on their use in context; they just list suggested options. However, in this case, BDAG has an interesting discussion about *koinonia* in 1 Corinthians 10:16. We will come back to this below.

When trying to determine the meaning of a word it is often helpful to study its use elsewhere, especially if it is used in the same book of the Bible under consideration. *Koinonia* is used elsewhere in 1 Corinthians at 1:9: 'God is faithful, through whom you were called into fellowship [*koinonia*] with His Son, Jesus Christ our Lord.' Anthony Thiselton argues for a vertical emphasis for *koinonia* here and translates it 'communal participation.' Commenting on this text, he says:

> Communal participation may seem to make heavy weather out of Gk. κοινωνίαν [*koinoniav*], which is usually translated fellowship. But the use of fellowship in church circles may convey an impression quite foreign to Paul's distinctive emphasis. He does not refer to a society or group of like-minded people, such as a Graeco-Roman *societas*. Certain specific uses of the word may have this meaning (e.g., Rom 15:27), but not this type of passage.

8. The Greek text does not contain an article before *koinonia*. There are times when the context warrants that a Greek noun without the article be translated with the article in English. If the reader is interested, consult Daniel B. Wallace's discussion on 'Absence of the Article' in his *Greek Grammar Beyond the Basics: An Exegetical Syntax of the New Testament* (Grand Rapids: Zondervan, 1996), 243ff. I wish the translators would have left *koinonia* on its own. But either way, it does not affect the meaning I will argue for below.

9. Walter Bauer, Revised and Edited by Frederick William Danker, Third Edition, *A Greek-English Lexicon of the New Testament and Other Early Christian Literature* (Chicago: The University of Chicago Press, 2000), 552-53.

> Normally in Paul the word means communal participation in that of which all participants are shareholders, or are accorded a common share. *It is not simply or primarily the experience of being together as Christians which is shared* [emphases added], but the status of being-in-Christ and of being shareholders in a sonship derived from the sonship of Christ. Just as the fellowship of the Holy Spirit (2 Cor. 13:13) means participating in the sharing out of the Spirit (which then secondarily gives rise to fellowship experience within a community), so the fellowship of his Son (1 Cor. 1:9) means communal participation in the sonship of Jesus Christ.[10]

Coming back to 1 Corinthians 10:16, Thiselton says that in this context, *koinonia* has a 'vertical and theological priority of emphasis over the horizontal and social'.[11] The Lord's Supper certainly has horizontal and social aspects to it (cf. 1 Cor. 11:17ff.), but in 1 Corinthians 10:16 in light of Paul's argument against idolatry (see my comments above and below), he is dealing with its *nature* in terms of its vertical aspect – *that which we commune with,* not the fact that *we* are communing. John Jefferson Davis says, '... participation implies living communion and actual personal contact.'[12] But actual personal contact with what or whom? Thiselton further adds it means 'having an active common share in the life, death, resurrection and presence of Jesus Christ as the Lord.'[13] Ernst Käsemann observes, 'Whatever objections may be raised against the term "Real Presence," it expresses what Paul wants to say.'[14] What these men are saying is that *koinonia* in

10. Anthony C. Thiselton, *The First Epistle to the Corinthians, A Commentary on the Greek Text, New International Greek Testament Commentary* (Grand Rapids: William B. Eerdmans Publishing Company, 2000), 104.

11. Thiselton, *First Corinthians*, 762.

12. John Jefferson Davis, *Worship and the Reality of God: An Evangelical Theology of Real Presence* (Downers Grove, IL: InterVarsity Press, 2010), 140.

13. As quoted by Davis, *Worship and the Reality of* God, 140.

14. Cf. Davis, *Worship and the Reality of God*, 140.

1 Corinthians 10:16 expresses a vertical, top-down reality, a reality connected to 'the blood' and 'the body of Christ'. Paul's emphasis is not that believers are together when they partake of the Lord's Supper (though that is true), it is that *koinonia* constitutes some sort of relationship with 'the blood' and 'the body of Christ'. This becomes clear when we understand the function of the two phrases modifying *koinonia*.

Koinonia in the Blood and Body of Christ?

What about the phrases after the noun *koinonia*? Could these help us with what Paul means? I think so. The KJV, NKJV, and ASV (1901) translate the phrases 'of the blood…of the body…' bringing out the genitive case articles ('the' [τοῦ]) and endings (αἵματος ['blood'] and σώματος ['body']) more than other versions. Inflected languages like Greek utilize different articles before words and endings to tell the reader how the word is functioning in a sentence and in our case in relation to that which it is modifying – *koinonia*. Notice that the phrases 'in the blood of Christ' and 'in the body of Christ' both modify *koinonia*. Because Paul uses the genitive case with 'the blood' and 'the body' I prefer the translation 'of the blood' and 'of the body'. This is the typical (though not exclusive) English translation of the genitive. However they translate, the more important issue is their function. The genitive case has various functions. Paul's use of it here could be what grammarians call the genitive of source. If so, we could read it this way, 'present communion derived from or dependent upon the blood and the body of Christ as its source'. The source of communion with Christ would be his blood and his body. Thiselton, quoting another scholar, says, 'A genitive following the word *koinonia* expresses … that of which one partakes ... the object shared.'[15] In this case, the objects shared are Christ's blood and Christ's body. BDAG's discussion (mentioned above) may help us at this point. While discussing *koinonia* when it is modified by a genitive case noun (or nouns as in our case), BDAG says it could mean '*the common possession* or *enjoyment of someth*[ing]'.[16] What is the thing or what are the things that are the common possession(s) or enjoyment of the Corinthians to which Paul is referring? The answer is 'the blood of Christ' and 'the body of Christ'. How do believers possess or enjoy 'the blood of Christ' and 'the body of Christ' through the Lord's Supper? We must look into this further.

The New International Dictionary of New Testament Theology says, '*koinonia* in 1 Corinthians 10:16 means "participation" in the body and blood of Christ and thus union with the *exalted* [emphasis mine] Christ.'[17] If Paul is talking about a *present communion* with 'the blood' and 'the body of Christ' and if Christ is no longer dying or dead, then the communion he is referring to is communion with the living, exalted Christ *now*. This is *present communion* with the living and exalted Lord of glory. The communion must be with the present benefits procured by his broken body and shed blood, for his body is no longer broken (it is glorified) and his blood has finished its shedding. Geoffrey B. Wilson agrees:

> The fact that Paul here refers to the sharing of the cup and the bread as a 'communion' of the blood and body of Christ proves that the Lord's Supper is something more than a memorial meal. For the believer shares in all *the benefits of Christ's sacrifice* [emphasis added] as he partakes of the tokens by which it is recalled but not re-enacted. 'The bread and wine are vehicles of the presence

15. Thiselton, *First Corinthians*, 104.

16. BDAG, 553.

17. J. Schattenmann, 'Fellowship, Have, Share, Participate' in NIDNTT, I:643.

> of Christ. ... Partaking of bread and wine is union (sharing) with the heavenly Christ' (F. Hauck, *TDNT*, Vol. 3, p. 805).[18]

If I had an earned reputation as a Greek scholar, I would be tempted to identify these phrases as eucharistic genitives of the real presence of the present benefits of Christ's death.[19]

Through the Lord's Supper, that which is signified by bread and wine ('the body' and 'the blood of Christ' as they benefit believers) is participated in by worthy partakers.

SHARERS IN THE ALTAR?

There are other questions that this text brings to mind, the answers of which help us understand Paul's argument. What about 1 Corinthians 10:18? Paul says, 'Look at the nation Israel [literally, 'Israel according to the flesh' (τὸν Ἰσραὴλ κατὰ σάρκα)]; are not those who eat the sacrifices sharers in the altar?' What does 'sharers in the altar' mean? It is of interest to note that Paul uses a different word here than he does in 10:16 for 'sharers' (κοινωνοὶ; a masculine noun and not simply the masculine form of *koinonia*. *Koinonia* has no masculine form.). Whether he is referring to ancient, Old Covenant Israel in the Old Testament or the Judaism of his own day, we know this much from his words, some sort of identity is established between those who offer sacrifices and the altar upon which those sacrifices are offered. But the identity between those who eat the sacrifices and the altar and those partaking of the Lord's Supper in 10:16 is not one and the same. Remember that Paul uses a different word here. He must be pointing to an analogous relationship between two things and not strict identity.[20] Thiselton says, '[Those who eat the sacrifices]

18. Geoffrey B. Wilson, *1 Corinthians: A Digest of Reformed Comment* (Edinburgh, Scotland and Carlisle, PA: The Banner of Truth Trust, 1978), 147.

19. To the multiplication of genitives there appears to be no end.

20. Cf. Maclean, *The Lord's Supper*, 32, where he says, 'Paul makes it clear that sharing

appropriate the reality or influence which the altar of sacrifice represents and conveys.'[21] Paul's point seems to be that 'to eat the food that had been offered in sacrifice was to participate in the cultic act of the sacrifice'.[22]

Sharers in demons?

Another question worth pursuing concerns 1 Corinthians 10:20. In 1 Corinthians 10:19-20, Paul says, 'What do I mean then? That a thing sacrificed to idols is anything, or that an idol is anything? *No*, but *I say* that the things which the Gentiles sacrifice, they sacrifice to demons and not to God; and I do not want you to become sharers in demons.' The words 'and not to God' are packed with implications. Remember, Paul is dealing with idolatry. In other words, the Gentile sacrificial meals were a form of idolatry. It is probably the case that Paul is alluding to Deuteronomy 32:17. There the Song of Moses recounts ancient Israel's idolatry in sacrificing to demons.[23] What does Paul mean by '... sharers in demons'? As in 1 Corinthians 10:18, he uses a different word than he does in 10:16 for 'sharers'. It must be that participating in pagan sacrificial meals opens one up to the influence of demons. This sharing involves some sort of contact with demons and is, thus, a form of idolatry (1 Cor. 10:14). This is why Paul says, 'You cannot drink the cup of the Lord and the cup of demons; you cannot partake of the table of the Lord and the table of demons' (1 Cor. 10:21). Regarding this verse, H. Bietenhard says:

---

in these temple meals involved communion with pagan gods (or the demonic powers behind these gods), *which was similar, in a way*, to the communion believers had with Christ at the Supper' (emphasis added).

21. Thiselton, *First Corinthians*, 772

22. Ciampa and Rosner, CNTUOT, 727.

23. See the discussion in Ciampa and Rosner, CNTUOT, 727-29.

> To sit down at the table of the *kyrios* [Lord] is to receive food from him and through it enter communion with him. Correspondingly, anyone who takes part in pagan sacrificial meals enters into communion with demons. ... The two activities are utterly incompatible.[24]

John Gill's comments are helpful at this juncture:

> The apostle's view in this instance, and his argument upon it, is this, that if believers, by eating the bread and drinking the wine in the Lord's supper, spiritually partake of Christ, of his body and of his blood, and have communion with him; then such who eat of things sacrificed unto idols, have in so doing communion with them, and partake of the table of devils, and so are guilty of idolatry, which he would have them avoid.[25]

I think Gill is right, as long as we understand that Paul is dealing with pagan sacrificial meals in 10:14-22.

The point of the text

The point being made from this text is that bread and wine are signs which signify *present* participation or *present* communion in the *present* benefits procured by Christ's body and blood. Grace procured by what Christ did for us becomes ours through the Lord's Supper. It is a means of grace. This is why the seventeenth-century English Particular Baptist Benjamin Keach, a signatory of the 2nd LCF, said, 'There is a mystical conveyance or communication of all Christ's blessed merits to our souls through faith held forth hereby, and in a glorious manner received, in the right participation of [the Lord's Supper].'[26] Likewise, in the

---

24. H. Bietenhard, 'Lord' in NIDNTT, 2:518.

25. John Gill, *Exposition of the Old and New Testaments*, Volume 8 (Paris, AR: The Baptist Standard Bearer, Inc., 1810, Reprinted 1989), 676.

26. Cited by Weaver in his unpublished, *Christ Spiritually Present and Believers Spiritually Nourished*, 24. Weaver is quoting Keach from *Preaching from the Types and Metaphors*

nineteenth century, C. H. Spurgeon said,'At this table, Jesus feeds us with his body and blood ...'[27]

Koinonia of the blood and body of Christ means spiritual nourishment is brought to souls. It is *present participation* in the *present benefits* of Christ's death for those properly partaking. In other words, the Lord's Supper is a means of grace. Paul brings up the nature of the Lord's Supper as a means of grace in this text to argue against participating in pagan sacrificial meals, which is idolatry. As Charles Hodge asserts,'It is here assumed that partaking of the Lord's Supper brings us into communion with Christ. If this be so, partaking of the table of demons must bring us into communion with demons. This is the apostle's argument.'[28] Any view of the Supper as only horizontal or memorial does not fit the context or prove the point of Paul's argument.

Practical considerations from 1 Corinthians 10:16

Communion or sharing is not horizontal, but vertical in 1 Corinthians 10:16. Since believers already have communion with Christ via faith (1 Cor. 1:9), the Lord's Supper must be viewed as a means to nurture what is already possessed. As Malcolm Maclean asserts,'This passage indicates that there is real fellowship between Christ and his people at the Supper.'[29] Though it is not a converting ordinance, the Supper is a sanctifying ordinance. Like the Word of God and prayer, it is a means through which grace comes to us from Christ. It is not a means of special grace, but a special means of grace.[30] Through the Lord's

---

of the Bible (Grand Rapids: Kregel Publications, 1972), 639.

27. C. H. Spurgeon, *Spurgeon's Sermons On The Death And Resurrection Of Jesus*. Accessed 26 June 2012. Available from http://books.google.com/.

28. Charles Hodge, *A Commentary on 1&2 Corinthians* (Edinburgh, Scotland and Carlisle, PA: The Banner of Truth Trust, 1857, Reprinted 1983), 185.

29. Maclean, *The Lord's Supper*, 33.

30. 'There is not a single benefit of grace that, withheld from us in the Word, is now imparted to believers in a special way by the sacrament. There is neither a separate baptismal grace nor a separate communion grace. The content of Word and sacrament is completely identical' (Bavinck, *Reformed Dogmatics*, IV:479).

Supper we receive something from Christ – the benefits of his body and blood. We are served something from Christ. The benefits of his body and blood are brought to us. As Bavinck said long ago, 'He not only gave himself *for* his own; he also gives himself *to* his own.'[31] We ought to look at the Supper as an event through which we receive and not only give. That which we receive is a top-down gift from heaven to earth, from our glorified Redeemer to us.

But how do the benefits of his death become present? How does that which resides in heaven (Christ's human nature and the benefits procured by his human nature) get to souls on the earth? That leads us into our next consideration. We will now look at two texts which speak about the ministry of the Holy Spirit in relation to our exalted Redeemer. Those texts are Ephesians 1:3 and 3:16-17. We will see that it is the role of the Holy Spirit to usher mediatorial, redemptive benefits from Christ in heaven to the souls of believers on the earth.

31. Bavinck, *Reformed Dogmatics*, IV:548.

3

Spiritual Blessings and the Holy Spirit

We will now look at Ephesians 1:3. Here is the NASB. 'Blessed *be* the God and Father of our Lord Jesus Christ, who has blessed us with every spiritual blessing in the heavenly *places* in Christ.' It will be argued that this text reveals to us the ministry of the Holy Spirit in the economy of redemption applied. The Spirit's function is to bring purchased blessings from our exalted Redeemer to the souls of believers.

Ephesians 1:3 in context

Ephesians 1:3 begins a section that ends at 1:14. It is the most glorious, doxologically – and soteriologically packed section of Paul's epistle to the Ephesians and probably of all his letters. Indeed, this may well be the highest biblical ground for worship prompted by the contemplation of what the triune God has done for believers from before the foundation of the world, what he has done in space and time in the world (culminating in the work of the Son), and finally what he does in bringing purchased redemption to the souls of men. Here God is blessed for trinitarian redemption purposed, purchased, and applied.

High-level observations

It will do us well to make some high-level observations before embarking upon a detailed exegesis of this verse. Before we do so, let us never forget that this section of Holy Scripture was written by a worshipping apostle in order that his readers might worship God for the reasons delineated in this wonderful passage.

First, we note that Paul departs from a somewhat normal pattern of a greeting followed by thanksgiving and prayer for the recipients. Harold W. Hoehner says, 'In this epistle he changes the order, for before he gives his thanksgiving [and prayer] in verses 15-23, he has in verses 3-14 a paean of praise for what God has done for the believer.'[1] This infuses Ephesians with a vertical, trinicentric perspective from the outset. The reason why Paul does this is not stated but may be inferred from background issues. It could be that the Ephesians were being entangled by their pagan background (cf. Acts 19) and needed to be reminded of what God had done for them and what he continually does in them (cf. also 1:19 and 3:16ff. and the power motif in various other places).

Second, the pericope has one all-controlling implied verb (i.e., the verb 'to be' in verse 3). The rest of the section is subordinate to the simple assertion of verse 3, 'Blessed *be* the God and Father of our Lord Jesus Christ. ...'

Third, prepositional phrases and participles play key roles in the development of the pericope. Here are a few examples:

1. Harold W. Hoehner, *Ephesians: An Exegetical Commentary* (Grand Rapids: Baker Academic, 2002), 153. 'Paean' is a fervent expression of joy or praise.

- The preposition ἐν ('in') occurs 15 times (vv. 3 [3x], 4 [2x], 6, 7, 9 [2x], 10 [2x], 11, 12, 13 [2x]) and plays a key role, especially concerning the doctrine of union with Christ (cf. vv. 3b, 4a, 7a).

- The preposition κατὰ ('according to') occurs five times (vv. 5, 7, 9, 11 [2x]).

- The participle ὁ εὐλογήσας ('who has blessed' of verse 3), which modifies 'the God and Father of our Lord Jesus Christ,' introduces us to the ways in which God the Father has blessed believers, which function as grounds or reasons why the Father is to be praised (i.e., 'with every spiritual blessing, in the heavenlies, in Christ').[2] It launches us into the blessings listed in verse 3 and is the syntactical basis from which we are introduced into the further blessings of verses 4-14. This is so because the 'just as' (καθὼς) of verse 4 is syntactically subordinate to ὁ εὐλογήσας ('who has blessed') in verse 3.

Fourth, this section (beginning at verse 3 and ending at verse 14) is one of the longer sentences in Ephesians. Hoehner claims that there are eight lengthy sentences in Ephesians (1:3-14, 15-23[3]; 2:1-7; 3:2-13, 14-19; 4:1-6, 11-16; 6:14-20).[4] Ephesians 1:3-14 has 202 words and has been the cause of one scholar claiming that it is 'the most monstrous sentence conglomeration (cannot even correctly call it a sentence) that he has ever found in the

2. I will show this in more detail below.

3. A case can be made that 1:15-23 should be extended into Chapter 2, maybe all the way to 2:10, making it the longest sentence in this epistle. Chapter 2 begins with καὶ ('and') which connects it with the previous section. That would make 2:1-10 a second illustration of the effective power of God that Paul wants his readers to know about (cf. 1:19ff.). The first illustration of this power is found in 1:20-23 – the power exerted in the exaltation of God's Son. The second illustration would be 2:1-10 – the power exerted in God's saints.

4. Hoehner, *Ephesians,* 153.

Greek language.'[5] It is of interest to note that three of these longer sentences in Ephesians deal with praise and/or prayer (1:3-14, 15-23 [2:10?]; and 3:14-19). It seems like Paul's soul gets 'caught up' while praising and petitioning God.

Fifth, though the sentence is syntactically complex, it does have indications of symmetry, development, and progress. This can be seen in the three refrains (1:6, 'to the praise of the glory of His grace' [εἰς ἔπαινον δόξης τῆς χάριτος αὐτοῦ], 1:12, 'to the praise of His glory' [εἰς ἔπαινον δόξης αὐτοῦ], and 1:14, 'to the praise of His glory' [εἰς ἔπαινον τῆς δόξης αὐτοῦ.]). Each of these refrains functions as an indicator of transition. As has been pointed out by many before, verses 4-6 concentrate on what God the Father has done, verses 7-12 on what God the Son has done, and verses 13-14 on what God the Spirit has done or does.

Symmetry, development, and progress can also be seen in the redemptive schema, framework, or pattern evident in the passage. The covenant of redemption (*pactum salutis*) can be seen in 1:4-6. The history of redemption (*historia salutis*) is alluded to in 1:7-12. The application of redemption (*ordo salutis*) is highlighted in 1:13-14. Let's look at each of these in order.

- *pactum salutis – 'covenant of redemption;* in Reformed federalism, the pretemporal, intratrinitarian agreement of the Father and the Son concerning the covenant of grace and its ratification in and through the work of the Son incarnate.'[6] The *pactum salutis* is evidenced in election by the Father in 1:4 that is said to be 'in Him' (i.e., in Christ). Election 'in Him' constitutes a pre-temporal, non-vital union with Christ in virtue of God's electing purpose and the Son's covenanted obedience. This reflects what Reformed theology has labeled the covenant of redemption. The same can be said about being '... predestined ... to adoption as sons ...' This, again, is a pre-

5. Hoehner, *Ephesians*, 153. Hoehner is referring to the opinion of Eduard Norden.

6. Muller, *Dictionary*, 217.

temporal appointment to a certain end which is reflective of the divine *pactum* because it is διὰ Ἰησοῦ Χριστοῦ ('through Jesus Christ') according to 1:5. The Father elects in the Son and predestinates those elected unto sonship through (διὰ) the Son, and he does both before the foundation of the world in virtue of the Son's covenanted obedience.

- *historia salutis* – the historical unfolding of salvation as found in the Holy Scriptures, culminating in the sufferings and glory of the Messiah. The *historia salutis* is evidenced by the historical accomplishment of τὴν ἀπολύτρωσιν διὰ τοῦ αἵματος αὐτοῦ ('redemption through His blood') in 1:7.

- *ordo salutis* – '*order of salvation;* a term applied to the temporal order of causes and effects through which the salvation of the sinner is accomplished; viz., calling, regeneration, adoption, conversion, faith, justification, renovation, sanctification, and perseverance.'[7] This refers to the order of the application of redemption. The *ordo salutis* is evidenced in believing the gospel and the sealing of the Holy Spirit of 1:13 (ἐν ᾧ καὶ πιστεύσαντες ἐσφραγίσθητε τῷ πνεύματι τῆς ἐπαγγελίας τῷ ἁγίῳ ['in whom also, having believed, you were sealed with the Holy Spirit of promise']), but also, as I will argue below, in 1:3.

Paul's redemptive structure or schema is clearly trinitarian.

The three refrains and the redemptive schema both indicate that though Paul might have been 'caught up' while writing, he did not lose his theological bearing. In fact, it is just the opposite. He was the most theological when he was the most adoring.

Broad outline of Ephesians 1:3-14

There are two main points in this section of Paul's letter. There is the controlling assertion concerning praise to God the Father

7. Muller, *Dictionary*, 215. I prefer the word 'applied' instead of 'accomplished'.

for redemptive blessings (1:3) and the multi-faceted elaboration concerning praise to God the Father for redemptive blessings (1:4-14). We will look at the first heading.

Exegesis of Ephesians 1:3

Here is the Greek text with my translation. Εὐλογητὸς ὁ θεὸς καὶ πατὴρ τοῦ κυρίου ἡμῶν Ἰησοῦ Χριστοῦ, ὁ εὐλογήσας ἡμᾶς ἐν πάσῃ εὐλογίᾳ πνευματικῇ ἐν τοῖς ἐπουρανίοις ἐν Χριστῷ ('Blessed be the God and Father of our Lord Jesus Christ, the One who has blessed us with every Spiritual blessing, in the heavenlies, in Christ').

This is the controlling assertion of the entire pericope (Eph. 1:3-14). The God and Father of our Lord Jesus Christ is being praised and is to be praised. It is of interest to note that there is evidence of trinitarianism in this verse: ὁ θεὸς καὶ πατὴρ ('the God and Father'/God the Father); ἐν Χριστῷ ('in Christ'/ God the Son]; and πνευματικῇ ('Spiritual'/God the Holy Spirit).[8] John Eadie says, '... And so the triune operation of the triune God is introduced: the Father who blesses – the Son, in whom those blessings are conferred – and the Spirit, by whose inner work they are enjoyed, and from whom they receive their distinctive epithet.'[9] We will look at the controlling assertion under three headings: its essence, its subject, and its ground.

The essence of the controlling assertion

The essence of the controlling assertion is seen in its first word – Εὐλογητὸς ('Blessed'). God the Father is being blessed by Paul and ought to be blessed by us. This word is used eight times in the New Testament and only of God (Mark 14:61; Luke 1:68;

8. We will discuss πνευματικῇ ('Spiritual') below.

9. John Eadie, *Ephesians* (Minneapolis: James & Klock Christian Publishing Company, 1883, Reprinted 1977), 18.

Rom. 1:25; 9:5; 2 Cor. 1:3; 11:31; Eph. 1:3; 1 Pet. 1:3). It introduces a eulogy, *berakah* (benediction patterned after the Old Testament), or anthem of praise in 2 Corinthians 1:3, here in Ephesians 1:3, and in 1 Peter 1:3. It means to speak well of, ascribe worth, value, or praise to someone. It has a rich Old Testament background (cf. Pss. 28:6; 31:21; 41:13; 119:12; 1 Chron. 29:10). Notice the LXX version of Psalm 28:6 [27:6 LXX], εὐλογητὸς κύριος ὅτι εἰσήκουσεν τῆς φωνῆς τῆς δεήσεώς μου ('Blessed be the Lord, because He has heard the voice of the supplication of me' [my translation]). In each of the texts cited above, the LXX fronts 'blessed' as it is in 2 Corinthians 1:3, Ephesians 1:3, and 1 Peter 1:3. The New Testament authors are, most likely, utilizing an ancient form of ascribing praise to God. Clinton E. Arnold even suggests that the use of an introductory *berakah* by Paul and Peter '... could mean that such an introductory exclamation of blessing was known and used in the worship of the early church.'[10]

As noted above, Εὐλογητὸς ('Blessed') is fronted in the text; it comes first. This is probably for emphasis. Edna Johnson comments: 'The occurrence of εὐλογητὸς 'blessed, praised' at the beginning of the verse, along with the use of cognate forms of this word three times in the verse, gives this concept emphasis. See εὐλογήσας "having blessed" and εὐλογίᾳ "blessing".'[11] God is to be blessed because he has so blessed us.

William J. Larkin identifies this word as a 'predicate adjective, with a passive verbal idea ...'[12] This makes it a verbal, predicate adjective. It is not the subject of the sentence and, since there is no

---

10. Clinton E. Arnold, *Exegetical Commentary on the New Testament: Ephesians* (Grand Rapids: Zondervan, 2010), 78.

11. Edna Johnson, *A Semantic Structural Analysis of Ephesians* (Dallas: SIL International, 2008), 41.

12. William J. Larkin, *Ephesians: A Handbook on the Greek Text* (Waco, TX: Baylor University Press, 2009), 5.

explicit verb, a verbal idea must be implied to help English readers make sense of it. A passive verbal idea means that the subject, 'the God and Father of our Lord Jesus Christ', is the one to be praised. It is probably best to imply an indicative of εἰμί ('to be').[13] Paul is not only praising God himself (i.e., worshipping while writing), he is promoting the worthiness of praising God to others. In the words of Peter T. O'Brien:

> ... as Paul begins his ... letter ..., he meditates on God's gracious purposes in Christ, and praise to God wells up within him. His desire is that adoration might overflow to his readers, so that they will be stimulated to respond as he does and give glory to God for all the gracious blessings to them.[14]

The subject of the controlling assertion

The subject of Ephesians 1:3 is ὁ θεὸς καὶ πατὴρ τοῦ κυρίου ἡμῶν Ἰησοῦ Χριστοῦ ('the God and Father of our Lord Jesus Christ'). He is the one who is to be blessed. There is some discussion about whether or not πατὴρ ('Father') is in apposition to ὁ θεὸς ('God') and if τοῦ κυρίου ἡμῶν Ἰησοῦ Χριστοῦ ('of our Lord Jesus Christ') modifies both terms. In the words of John Eadie, this would mean that 'the Divine Being is both God and Father of our Lord Jesus Christ'.[15] It seems best to take it as Eadie says. The genitive phrase ('of our Lord Jesus Christ') modifies both nominatives ('the God and Father').[16] This does not necessitate ὁ θεὸς ('the God') and πατὴρ ('Father') being in apposition to each other. In fact, Larkin suggests that this is an example of the Granville Sharp rule: 'The article before the first but not the second of two personal, singular, non-proper nouns linked by καὶ

13. Larkin, *Ephesians*, 5-6.

14. Peter T. O'Brien, *The Letter to the Ephesians*, Pillar New Testament Commentary (Grand Rapids: William B. Eerdmans Publishing Company, 1999), 92-93.

15. Eadie, *Ephesians*, 11.

16. Most commentators take it this way.

...indicates the second noun refers to the same person mentioned by the first noun...'[17] The person who is God or divine is also in a special, twofold relationship with 'our Lord Jesus Christ.' He is his God and his Father.

Considering the Old Testament background of the *berakah*, it is important to note that 'the God of Abraham, Isaac, and Jacob,' 'the God of Israel' is now also 'the God and Father of our Lord Jesus Christ.' Ancient Israel had God as its God and Father (cf. Exod. 4:22-23, '... Israel is My son, My firstborn ... Let My son go that he may serve me ...'). In the case of ancient Israel, God's son failed to obey his vocation and broke the covenant, just like God's primal son, Adam (cf. Hos. 6:7 with Luke 3:38). In the case of God's unique, eternal Son in his incarnate state, he not only did not break the covenant (like Adam and Israel), he was rewarded for his obedience and, as a result, covenantal blessings are 'lavished' (Eph. 1:8) upon those for whom he came to obey.[18]

The ground of the controlling assertion

The ground of the controlling assertion of 1:3 is found at 1:3c (ὁ εὐλογήσας ἡμᾶς ... ('who has blessed us ...'). Paul introduces us to a participial clause, ὁ εὐλογήσας ἡμᾶς ... ('who has blessed us ...'), which is modifying ὁ θεὸς καὶ πατὴρ ('the God and Father'). How is this clause functioning? We will discuss this clause under these two headings: 1) the statement of its ground and 2) the elements of its ground.

The statement of its ground is seen in the words ὁ εὐλογήσας ἡμᾶς ('who has blessed us'). As noted in the discussion above, this

17. Larkin, *Ephesians*, 6. Larkin points his readers to Wallace's discussion of this rule in his *Greek Grammar Beyond the Basics*, 271.

18. This is a good reminder that while reading Paul, we need to make sure we read him with theologically informed Old Testament eyes.

clause introduces us to the reasons or grounds for praising God the Father. Why is this? O'Brien notes that in Old Testament *berakahs* the name of God is typically followed by 'a participial clause which gives the reasons for praising God ...'[19] In Ephesians 1:3 (and 2 Cor. 1:3 and 1 Peter 1:3), '... the ground for blessing God is similarly expressed by a participial clause.'[20] Why is God the Father blessed? Because he has blessed us. But how has he blessed us? This brings us to the elements for which we ought to praise the Father.

The elements of its ground are seen in three prepositional phrases which modify the participial clause: *ἐν πάσῃ εὐλογίᾳ πνευματικῇ ἐν τοῖς ἐπουρανίοις ἐν Χριστῷ* ('**with** every Spiritual blessing, **in** the heavenlies, **in** Christ'). How are we to view these phrases? Are they all coordinately subordinate to the participle ὁ εὐλογήσας ἡμᾶς ('the one who blessed')? Are the latter two subordinate to the first? There are various plausible options. I think it best to view each prepositional phrase as coordinate among themselves and subordinate to the participle. This would mean that Paul is giving us three reasons or grounds for God to be praised by believers – 1) because he blessed us 'with every Spiritual blessing', 2) because he blessed us 'in the heavens', and 3) because he blessed us 'in Christ'. Several commentators take this view – Lincoln, O'Brien, Arnold, Thielman. Here is a diagram of the clause which may help to see its structure:

ὁ εὐλογήσας ἡμᾶς

1. ἐν πάσῃ εὐλογίᾳ πνευματικῇ
2. ἐν τοῖς ἐπουρανίοις
3. ἐν Χριστῷ

19. O'Brien, *Ephesians*, 94. He cites Ps. 72:18.

20. O'Brien, *Ephesians*, 95. Cf. Hoehner, *Ephesians*, 165.

the One who has blessed us

1. with every Spiritual blessing
2. in the heavenlies
3. in Christ

Assuming that the phrases are to be understood this way, this gives us three reasons why God the Father is to be blessed (i.e., praised, worshipped, adored) by those he blesses (i.e., confers benefits, favors, or gifts upon). God the Father is to be praised by believers for three reasons.

The first reason God the Father is worthy of praise is due to the fact that he has blessed believers *ἐν πάσῃ εὐλογίᾳ πνευματικῇ* ('with every [or "all"] Spiritual blessings'). The adjective *πάσῃ* 'all') is modifying the noun εὐλογίᾳ ('blessing') and indicates quantity. 'Every' spiritual blessing God has for believers has come (or will come) to them. God is not a stingy giver. He is to be praised due to the quantity of blessings conferred.

What do we make of the second word modifying εὐλογίᾳ ('blessing') – *πνευματικῇ* ('Spiritual')? I think it best to take this as a reference to the bearer of God's blessings, the One appointed to bring the fruits of Christ's redemptive labors to the souls of men – i.e., the Holy Spirit. This adjective is used twenty-six times in the New Testament. All but two uses (1 Pet. 2:5 [2x]) are found in Paul. It often refers to that which pertains to the Spirit of God (cf. Rom. 1:11 and Col. 1:9). In both of these cases 'spiritual' refers to that which is *produced by* or *brought to our souls by* the Holy Spirit. In 1 Corinthians 2:14-16 and 3:1-4, Paul contrasts the spiritual person with the natural/soulish person and the spiritual person with the fleshly person. In both cases 'the spiritual person is the one who knows and wants that which is of the Spirit of God.'[21] In 1 Corinthians 15:44-46 there is a contrast between the spiritual body – animated by the Spirit of God and fit for the resurrected and eternal state (i.e., the age to come) – and the natural/soulish body which is fit for this age alone. Eadie says, 'But in all other passages where, as in this clause, the word is used to qualify Christian men, or Christian blessings, its ruling reference is plainly to the Holy Spirit.'[22] He then cites eleven Pauline texts and concludes, 'Therefore the prevailing usage of the New Testament warrants us in saying, that these blessings are termed spiritual from their connection with the Holy Spirit.'[23] Here, in Ephesians 1:3, it refers to the Spirit of God as the bearer of God the Father's blessings procured for us by the blood of Christ (Eph. 1:7). These blessings are both *brought by* and *wrought by* the Spirit. Thielman agrees, when he says, '"Spiritual blessings," therefore, are the benefits that come as gracious gifts from the Spirit of God ...'[24] Commenting upon 'every spiritual blessing,' Eadie says:

> The circle is complete. No needed blessing is wanted – nothing that God has promised, or Christ has secured ... And those blessings are all in the hand of the Spirit. Christianity is the dispensation of the Spirit, and as its graces are inwrought by Him, they are all named 'spiritual' after Him.[25]

The second reason God the Father is worthy of praise is due to the fact that he has blessed believers ἐν τοῖς ἐπουρανίοις ('in the heavenlies'). This phrase refers to the sphere of the plenteous blessings – 'the heavenlies' – or maybe better to the dimension

21. Hoehner, *Ephesians*, 167.

22. Eadie, *Ephesians*, 14.

23. Eadie, *Ephesians*, 14.

24. Frank Thielman, *Ephesians*, Baker Exegetical Commentary on the New Testament (Grand Rapids: Baker Academic, 2010), 47.

25. Eadie, *Ephesians*, 14.

of existence in which believers experience spiritual blessings.[26] Heaven is that place where God's presence is manifested intensely. With reference to the intermediate state of believers, heaven is that, plus a state of existence qualitatively different than that which we experience presently on the earth. However, I do not think Paul is reserving the blessings of the heavenly state exclusively for the intermediate and/or eternal states. Charles Hodge says, '... these blessings pertain to that heavenly state into which the believer is [not "will be"] introduced.'[27] This is probably best understood in an already/not-yet eschatological sense – the heavenly realm as a state of existence. And the heavenly realm as a state of existence for believers on the earth is the age-to-come eclipsing this age in relation to the sufferings and glory of Christ and in relation to the experience of believers by the ministry of the Holy Spirit. Andrew T. Lincoln says:

> ... the heavenly realms in Ephesians are to be seen in the perspective of the age to come, which has been inaugurated by God raising Christ from the dead and exalting him to his right hand. ... the blessings of salvation [believers] have received from God link [them] to the heavenly realm. The blessings can be said to be in the heavenly realms, yet they are not viewed as treasure stored up for future appropriation, but as benefits belonging to believers now.[28]

The heavenly realm (or the heavenlies) is the age-to-come and that age has come in relation to the sufferings and glory of Christ. O'Brien says:

> In the heavenly realms is bound up with the divine saving

26. Thielman, *Ephesians*, 47.

27. Charles Hodge, *A Commentary on the Epistle of the Ephesians* (New York: Hodder & Stoughton, 1856), 29

28. Andrew T. Lincoln, *Word Biblical Commentary, Volume 42, Ephesians* (Dallas: Word Books, Publisher, 1990), 21.

> events and is to be understood within a Pauline eschatological perspective. In line with the Jewish two-age structure heaven is seen from the perspective of the age to come, which has now been inaugurated by the death and resurrection of the Lord Jesus Christ.[29]

These blessings are not stored up for us in heaven for the future. They are not blessings to be enjoyed once we get where Christ is. Instead, it is as if heaven has been and is being brought to our souls by the Holy Spirit (through the means of grace) due to the work of Christ in accordance with the Father's electing and predestinating purpose. Eadie says:

> Now the gospel, or the Mediatorial reign, is 'the kingdom of heaven.' That kingdom or reign of God is 'in us,' or among us. Heaven is brought near to man through Jesus Christ. Those spiritual blessings conferred on us create heaven within us ...; for wherever the light and love of God's presence are to be enjoyed, there is heaven. If such blessings are the one Spirit's inworking, – that Spirit who in God's name 'takes of the things that are Christ's and shows them unto us,' – then His influence diffuses the atmosphere of heaven around us.[30]

The age-to-come has eclipsed this age and believers taste of that world in this world by the ministry of the Holy Spirit – the bearer of heavenly, age-to-come blessings in this age.

The third reason God the Father is worthy of praise is due to the fact that he has blessed us ἐν Χριστῷ ('in Christ'). This prepositional phrase is a common one in Paul. It (or a slight variant of it) is used eleven times in this passage alone. It is the third and final prepositional phrase in a series highlighting reasons why believers are to bless God the Father. It refers to the fact of incorporation and solidarity in Christ. It is due to union

29. O'Brien, *Ephesians*, 97.

30. Eadie, *Ephesians*, 16-17.

with Christ (i.e., incorporation) that all saints (i.e. solidarity) get 'every spiritual blessing in the heavenlies ...' The concepts of incorporation and solidarity have their biblical tap-roots in the Garden of Eden in the first man, Adam (1 Cor. 15:22). But unlike the first man (God's son [Luke 3:38]) and God's corporate son (Old Covenant Israel), the last Adam (God's unique, eternal Son, who became man for us and for our salvation) does not fail his probation. He passes probation and the Holy Spirit confers upon those he represented all the merited blessings procured through suffering obedience that Adam (and Old Covenant Israel) failed to attain. Adam (and all in him) and Israel were cursed for their disobedience. Christ was cursed for our disobedience but raised for our justification, which finds as its basis his obedience for us. It is because believers are in union with Christ that they get what the Holy Spirit brings to their souls – the benefits of Christ's body and blood. There are, therefore, no curses for those who are in Christ Jesus. All we get are blessings, lavished blessings (Eph. 1:8), due to union with Christ.

How does all this relate to the Lord's Supper?

Ephesians 1:3 helps us understand *that* and *how* God brings grace to men. God the Father is to be praised by believers due to the ministry of the Holy Spirit in ushering into our souls soteric-eschatological blessings that have been purchased for us by Christ. A taste of heaven is brought to the souls of believers by the Holy Spirit. Grace is glory begun or glory in the bud. The Holy Spirit brings purchased blessings from the mediator between God and men, our Lord Jesus Christ, who is exalted at the right hand of the Father in heaven. Ephesians teaches that the Holy Spirit brings heavenly blessings to the souls of believers (1:3). He does this due to the fact that Christ procured these blessings through his blood (1:7). Redemption accomplished means blessings for those redeemed. Redemption benefits the redeemed in this life and in the life-to-come. The benefits of redemption through Christ's blood are brought to the souls of elect sinners. This is the work of the Holy Spirit. The benefits of Christ's blood and body (1 Cor. 10:16) are spiritual blessings (Eph. 1:3), brought to souls by the Spirit of Christ. Through the Lord's Supper, communion with Christ and the benefits of his blood and body takes place. This communion is effected by the Holy Spirit, the bearer of blessings from the Father because of the work of the Son. This is how the Lord's Supper is a means of grace. It was instituted by Christ and is blessed by the Spirit of Christ to the nourishment of our pilgrim souls. Just as our Lord Jesus Christ is the mediator between God and men (1 Tim. 2:5), the Holy Spirit is the 'mediator' between our exalted Redeemer and elect sinners on the earth through the means of grace. The Spirit is the effective agent between our Lord Jesus in heaven and us – the go-between, intercessor, intermediary, intermediator. As Sinclair Ferguson says, '... in the Supper, the Spirit comes to "close the gap" as it were between Christ in heaven and the believer on earth, and to give communion with the exalted Saviour.'[31] Through the Lord's Supper, God does something. As Bavinck says, 'Of primary importance in the Lord's Supper is what God does, not what we do. The Lord's Supper is above all a gift of God, a benefit of Christ, a means of communicating his grace.'[32] Grace from Christ in heaven is communicated to believers on the earth by the Holy Spirit through the Lord's Supper. The Holy Spirit takes the things of the exalted Christ and discloses them to believers (John 16:14).

31. Sinclair B. Ferguson, *The Holy Spirit* (Downers Grove, IL: InterVarsity Press, 1996), 203.

32. Bavinck, *Reformed Dogmatics*, IV:567.

He brings purchased blessings special delivery to souls from the Lord Christ. Ephesians 1:3 supplies us with the theological mechanics which are assumed by 1 Corinthians 10:16. When we take the Supper, it is the Spirit of Christ who brings the benefits of Christ to the people of Christ. Praise God from whom all blessings flow. Praise Father, Son, and Holy Ghost!

4

Spiritual Invigoration through Prayer

I have attempted to establish that the Holy Spirit is the divine agent commissioned by the Father to deliver redemptive or spiritual blessings to the souls of men on the earth (Eph. 1:3).[1] His work in the application of redemption is to usher that which was procured by Christ in the history of redemption to those chosen in him (Eph. 1:3, 4, 7, 13-14) and predestinated to sonship through him (Eph. 1:5). This is his work for us in the economy of redemption. This is why it is the Spirit who effects communion between believers and the exalted Christ through the Lord's Supper (1 Cor. 10:16) and why it is a means of grace. The Lord's Supper is one of the delivery systems ordained by Christ for the communication of the benefits of his death to his people. The ministry of the Holy Spirit in relation to the means of grace is an important aspect in understanding the Supper as one of those means. But as was stated above, the means of grace include prayer, and since prayer is conducted during the Lord's

1. Actually, the Spirit is sent by both the Father and the Son (John 14:26; 15:26; 16:7; Acts 2:33 [Luke 24:49]; Eph. 1:3). We will discuss this briefly in the last chapter.

Supper (1 Cor. 11:23-25), it is proper for us to consider it in our discussion. In light of this, to better understand the Supper as a means of grace, understanding prayer as a means and the ministry of the Spirit through prayer in relation to the blessings that are ours in Christ can fill in a theological gap which may still be lingering in the minds of some readers.

Prayer is both a spiritual privilege and duty of the Christian. It is the breathing-out of the soul its praise to God and its requests for things perceived as necessary for one's own life or the life of others. Prayer is a great privilege. The believer in Christ has God as his audience during prayer. Prayer, as we will see shortly, is a means through which God brings needed things to souls. Prayer is a means of grace.

Context and structure of Ephesians 3:14-21

Ephesians 3:14-21 contains Paul's second prayer in Ephesians. He announces this prayer explicitly in 3:14, 'For this reason I bow my knees before the Father.' He identifies to whom he is praying in 3:14b, 15, '... the Father, from whom every family in heaven and on earth derives its name.' The content of his prayer is found in 3:16-19 and its conclusion, a doxology, in 3:20-21.

The structure of this pericope is somewhat difficult to determine.[2] It hinges upon three ἵνα (*hina*) clauses. Though there is disagreement as to how these clauses function, I think a good case can be made for a threefold prayer.[3] The clauses under consideration are in 3:16, 'that He would grant you ...' (ἵνα δῷ

2. This passage has a web of syntactical difficulties in it. Having worked my way through the Greek text and many commentaries over the years, I am aware of the fact that readers may not agree with every syntactical decision I have made. I take some comfort in the fact that no two commentaries on Ephesians that I am aware of agree on all the tough syntactical and semantic calls demanded by the text. Not only is the syntax complex and difficult to sort out, the meaning seems just as allusive at times.

3. As will be shown below, the NKJV reflects this view.

ὑμῖν), 3:17b-18a, '*and* that you, ..., may be able to comprehend ...' (ἵνα ἐξισχύσητε καταλαβέσθαι [The Greek text has ἵνα (*hina*) at the beginning of verse 18]), and in the middle of 3:19, 'that you may be filled ...' (ἵνα πληρωθῆτε). These three ἵνα (*hina*) clauses function as indicators of the threefold content of Paul's prayer.[4]

Notice at 3:16, where Paul introduces us to the first part of his petition with the words ἵνα δῷ ὑμῖν ('that He would grant you'). This clause is subordinate to the main verb found in 3:1, κάμπτω ('I bow'). It indicates the reason or purpose for which Paul bows his 'knees before the Father.' The implied subject of the verb in this clause is clearly 'the Father' of 3:1. The Father is the granter of that which Paul wants granted to the Ephesians.

The NASB's 'so that' of 3:17a is not another ἵνα (*hina*) clause indicator. It is the beginning of an infinitival clause (κατοικῆσαι τὸν Χριστὸν ['so that Christ may dwell']). It is subordinate to verse 16. It most likely indicates the purpose, result, or goal of 'be[ing] strengthened with power through His Spirit in the inner man' (3:16b).[5]

One of the difficulties with determining how the three ἵνα (*hina*) clauses function comes to the surface at the end of verse 17 and beginning of verse 18. The NASB translates 3:17b-18a as '*and* that you, being rooted and grounded in love, may be able to comprehend ...' Notice that 'and' is in italics and followed by 'that.' As noted above, the Greek text has 'that' (ἵνα [*hina*]) at the beginning of verse 18. The reason why translators insert '*and* that you' at this point is because it is thought that 'being rooted and grounded in love' at the end of verse 17 goes with the ἵνα (*hina*) clause of verse 18.[6] Whether or not this is correct, I take it

4. Even if Paul's prayer is not threefold, it does not affect the meaning of 3:16-17.

5. See the discussion in Glenn H. Graham, *An Exegetical Summary of Ephesians*, Second Edition 2008 (Dallas: SIL International, 1997), 249-50. He lists at least seven commentaries that take this view.

6. I will argue below that 'being rooted and grounded in love' should be taken with what precedes not with what follows.

that this second ἵνα (*hina*) introduces us to a second clause which functions as the second part of Paul's petition.[7]

The third ἵνα (*hina*) clause is found in the middle of verse 19, 'that you may be filled up to all the fullness of God' (ἵνα πληρωθῆτε εἰς πᾶν τὸ πλήρωμα τοῦ θεοῦ.). The function of this clause is also debated. Is it a third petition or does it relate directly and subordinately to the second petition and maybe even the first?

The NKJV may help us at this point. It inserts semicolons immediately prior to the word 'that' in the middle of verses 17 and 19. This indicates transition from one petition to the next. Here is the NKJV:

> [16]**that** He would grant you, according to the riches of His glory, to be strengthened with might through His Spirit in the inner man, [17]that Christ may dwell in your hearts through faith; **that** you, being rooted and grounded in love, [18]may be able to comprehend with all the saints what *is* the width and length and depth and height – [19]to know the love of Christ which passes knowledge; **that** you may be filled with all the fullness of God. (Eph. 3:16-19 NKJV; emphasis added)[8]

Understood this way, Paul's petition has three aspects or parts. I prefer this understanding of the text.[9]

---

7. Cf. the discussion on the various options in Graham, *Ephesians*, 254-55.

8. Notice that the NKJV does not begin verse 19 with 'and' as does the KJV, ASV (1901), NASB, ESV, and NIV. Though there is no 'and' (καὶ) in the Greek text at this point, the particle τε (*te*) is present after the first word 'to know.' The words 'to know' translate the infinitive γνῶναί which is connected to 'that you, ..., may be able to comprehend ...' (ἵνα ἐξισχύσητε καταλαβέσθαι) of verse 18. The postpositive particle τε is not always translated. Here it most likely functions adjunctively, indicating a closer connection than καὶ ('and'). Either Paul wanted the Ephesians to 'be able' to do two things, 'to comprehend' and 'to know' or he wanted them to 'be able to comprehend' in order 'to know' or 'to know ...' could be epexegetical ('[that is] to know ...'), functioning as the content of what he wants them to be able to comprehend (NKJV?). This much is clear; τε indicates some sort of sameness and continuation of thought with that which precedes it. Cf. Larkin, *Ephesians*, 64.

9. Cf. the discussion on the various options in Graham, *Ephesians*, 260 and Larkin, *Ephesians*, 59, 61, 63, and 64. Larkin holds the three-petition view. Either way, it does

Assuming the three-petition view, Paul prays for spiritual invigoration in 3:16-17, spiritual education in 3:18-19a, and spiritual saturation in 3:19b. Most likely, we are to understand a progression from the first to the third. The second petition is dependent upon the first and the third is dependent upon both. What is very clear is that Paul, in reviewing his prayer for the Ephesians, ends up teaching us something about his view of prayer as a means of grace. He is praying that the Father in heaven would do something to elect and believing souls on the earth.

Paul's prayer for spiritual invigoration

We will look at the first part of Paul's prayer in Ephesians 3:16-17. The rest of the passage could also be used to illustrate what 3:16-17 does – that prayer is a means of grace – but for sake of space I will not discuss it in detail. Every phrase and clause of these verses is important for our discussion. They teach us what Paul thought occurred (or could occur) as a result of prayer. It will become clear as we work our way through this text that prayer, in the mind of the apostle, is a means of grace.

The benevolent provider of Paul's prayer

First, notice the benevolent provider of Paul's prayer: ἵνα δῷ ('that He would grant'). The 'He' refers back to 'the Father' (v. 14). The word 'grant' here means to give or bestow upon freely, gladly, and yet sovereignly. Our heavenly Father is pleased to bestow gifts upon the souls of those who do not earn or deserve them. Paul is praying to the Father. He is asking the Father to give something to the Ephesians. Paul's assumption is that God, our Father, works through the prayers of believers. Our Father has a large heart for his children. He is pleased to grant what we really need.

---

not change the fact that at 3:16 Paul gives us the first element of his prayer and, as argued above, at verse 17b or 18a, he most likely transitions to his second.

The beneficiary recipients of Paul's prayer

Notice second, the beneficiary recipients of Paul's prayer: ὑμῖν ('you' [literally 'to you']). Paul believes in a God who acts on behalf of men or for the benefit of souls on the earth. He prays specifically for particular persons, assuming that the Father of believers not only hears prayer but grants requests made by his children. Prayer is a means through which God gives things to men. Individual souls are the beneficiary recipients of prayer.

The unbounded measure of Paul's prayer

Third, notice the unbounded measure of Paul's prayer: κατὰ τὸ πλοῦτος τῆς δόξης αὐτοῦ ('according to the riches of His glory'). This phrase depicts the measure with which Paul desires God to give to these Ephesians. Eadie says:

> ... He gives like Himself, not grudgingly or in tiny portions, as if He were afraid to exhaust His riches, or even suspected them to be limited in their contents. There is no fastidious scrupulosity or anxious frugality on the part of the Divine Benefactor. His bounty proclaims His conscious possession of immeasurable resources. He bestows according to the riches of His glory – His own infinite fulness.[10]

Paul recognizes the great need the Ephesians have and the great resources God has to meet their needs and his prayer reflects this. God has all we need stored up for us in heaven.

The specific essence of Paul's prayer

Fourth, notice the specific essence of Paul's prayer: δυνάμει κραταιωθῆναι ('to be strengthened with power'). This means to fortify, to invigorate with strength. We might say that Paul is praying that God would give the Ephesians infused invigoration

10. Eadie, *Ephesians*, 243.

of soul. Paul asks for something to be brought to souls. He wants these souls to be changed by his benevolent Father.

The divine deliverer of Paul's prayer

Fifth, notice the divine deliverer of Paul's prayer: διὰ τοῦ πνεύματος αὐτοῦ ('through His Spirit'). The phrase διὰ τοῦ πνεύματος αὐτοῦ ('through His Spirit') indicates that the Spirit is the means of deliverance of the things granted by the Father. This is seen by the fact that the preposition διὰ (*dia*) finds as its object a genitive case noun τοῦ πνεύματος ('the Spirit'). The Holy Spirit (i.e., the Spirit of the Father in this text) is the divine means through which spiritual invigoration comes to souls on the earth. It is the ministry of the Holy Spirit to invigorate Christians, to infuse them with power, to deliver blessings from heaven to earth. The Spirit of God is the divine agent through which power comes to souls through prayer. As Eadie says, '[The Holy Spirit] has free access to man's spirit to move it as He may, and it is His peculiar function in the scheme of mercy to apply to the heart the spiritual blessings provided by Christ.'[11] 'He will take of mine and will disclose it to you' (John 16:14), Jesus said.

The desired location of Paul's prayer

Sixth, notice the desired location of Paul's prayer: εἰς τὸν ἔσω ἄνθρωπον ('in the inner man'). This refers to the soul, the aspect of our being that cannot be seen, cannot be physically touched, but can be weak and feeble, be strengthened with power, be invigorated or infused with strength from heaven. Prayer is a means through which the Father grants the Holy Spirit to bring spiritual invigoration to souls.

---

11. Eadie, *Ephesians*, 244.

The intended result or goal of Paul's prayer

Seventh, notice the intended result or goal of Paul's prayer: κατοικῆσαι τὸν Χριστὸν διὰ τῆς πίστεως ἐν ταῖς καρδίαις ὑμῶν ('so that Christ may dwell in your hearts through faith'). Since the Ephesians were already believers (Eph. 1:13), Christ already dwelt in their hearts through faith. Paul teaches elsewhere that Christ is in believers or those who possess saving faith (Rom. 8:10; 2 Cor. 13:3, 5; Gal. 2:20; and Col. 1:27). Commenting on our text, Frank Thielman says:

> Paul does not imply by this that Christ is absent from their hearts. They could hardly be sealed by the Spirit (1:13), united with Christ in his resurrection and exaltation (2:5-6), and incorporated into the place where God dwells ... by his Spirit (2:22) yet fail to have Christ dwelling in their hearts.[12]

But Paul prays that they would be strengthened *so that* Christ *may* dwell in their hearts through faith. What does this mean? Paul uses an aorist infinitive here: κατοικῆσαι ('may dwell'). One of the functions of the aorist tense is to put the stress on the action as a whole. This is determined by its use in context and not by the form itself. There are many times when the aorist is used and the duration envisioned is not a point in time but the action as a whole. For example, notice John 2:20, which says, 'The Jews then said, "It took forty-six years to build this temple, and will You raise it up in three days?"' The verb translated 'to build' is in the aorist tense and yet it envisions a 46-year period. The same can be illustrated by Galatians 1:18. 'Then three years later I went up to Jerusalem to become acquainted with Cephas, and stayed with him fifteen days.' The verb translated 'stayed' is an aorist that covers a period of fifteen days. Lincoln says of κατοικῆσαι ('may dwell'), 'The verb indicates that the focus of

12. Thielman, *Ephesians*, 230-31.

the prayer request is not on an initial reception of Christ but on believers' experience of his constant presence.'[13] This is probably what grammarians call a constative aorist. The stress of the verb is on the action as a whole. Therefore, the indwelling of Christ can be realized by Christians at different levels and at different times, though it is a constant reality. On the one hand, Christ dwells in all believers. On the other hand, through the ministry of the Spirit, who strengthens or nourishes faith, faith becomes a means (διὰ τῆς πίστεως ['through faith']; *dia* with the genitive case expressing means) through which that dwelling is known. It is the means through which the knowledge or sense of his presence is enhanced in our hearts. We are enabled to believe that which is always true of us (i.e., Christ dwells in us) by the work of the Spirit in us as a result of prayer to the Father. Both initial (saving) and subsequent (sanctifying) faith are results of the Spirit's work in us.

The goal of Paul's prayer is that the Ephesians' faith might be refreshed, renewed, strengthened, or nourished by the Spirit of the Father (and the Son) so that they might know the experiential presence of Christ, or 'a growing experience of the nearness of the Lord'.[14] The invigoration of soul brought to believers by the Spirit from the Father results in a deeper awareness of the constant dwelling of Christ in the heart through faith. Prayer is a means through which our faith is both sustained and developed.

The parenthetical reminder of Paul's prayer

And *finally*, notice the parenthetical reminder of Paul's prayer: ἐν ἀγάπῃ ἐρριζωμένοι καὶ τεθεμελιωμένοι ('being rooted and grounded in love'). I say parenthetical reminder because I think this compound participial clause is best understood as standing

13. Lincoln, *Ephesians*, 206.

14. Arnold, *Ephesians*, 211.

somewhat on its own as an interjection[15] and translated as 'having already been [and continually being] rooted and grounded in love'. Both participles are perfect passives, indicating past action with abiding results. But due to their nominative case endings it is difficult to find that which they modify syntactically.[16] Though many take them with the clause that begins in 3:18,[17] the ἵνα (*hina*) there introduces us to a new clause as it does in 3:19. The three-petition view I advocate understands each ἵνα (*hina*) as the beginning (it comes first) and, therefore, an indicator of a new clause. Paul appears to be reminding the Ephesians that they are already rooted and grounded in the love that God has for them in Christ. His desire is that their faith would be enhanced by the ministry of the Spirit. This would confirm the fact that Christ already dwelt in them but Paul wanted that to be further enhanced in their understanding. In effect, he is saying, 'You are and always will be rooted and grounded in God's love for you, but I want the Father to give you strength through his Spirit, in the inner man, so that what is true of you – Christ dwells in you – will be constantly known by you through faith.'

Other texts in Paul which illustrate prayer as a means of grace

There are many other texts in Paul and the rest of Scripture which illustrate prayer as a means of grace. I will list only four from Paul's letters, making brief comments along the way. With

15. Cf. Thielman, *Ephesians*, 232 for this view and the other commentaries consulted above for the various views and the complexity of this construction.

16. For current discussion of the various views and the difficulties involved with identifying a precise syntactical function, cf. Arnold, *Ephesians*, 212-14 and Thielman, *Ephesians*, 231-33. I once held that the participles modified ὑμῖν ('you') of verse 16, a dative case plural personal pronoun. However, as Thielman points out, if that were so, the participles would not be in the nominative case (Thielman, *Ephesians*, 231).

17. Cf., however, Graham, *Ephesians*, 252, where he lists ten commentaries and two versions which take the participles with the preceding in 3:16-17.

the discussion above in our minds, it becomes quite easy to see that Paul believed prayer to be a means of grace.

Consider Romans 15:30-31:

> 'Now I urge you, brethren, by our Lord Jesus Christ and by the love of the Spirit, to strive together with me in your prayers to God for me, that I may be rescued from those who are disobedient in Judea, and *that* my service for Jerusalem may prove acceptable to the saints.'

Paul's preservation and acceptable service are seen as dependent upon on what God is pleased to do through the prayers of his people.

Also, 2 Corinthians 1:8-11:

> '[8]For we do not want you to be unaware, brethren, of our affliction which came *to us* in Asia, that we were burdened excessively, beyond our strength, so that we despaired even of life; [9]indeed, we had the sentence of death within ourselves so that we would not trust in ourselves, but in God who raises the dead; [10]who delivered us from so great a *peril of* death, and will deliver *us*, He on whom we have set our hope. And He will yet deliver us, [11]you also joining in helping us through your prayers, so that thanks may be given by many persons on our behalf for the favor bestowed on us through *the prayers of* many.'

Paul viewed prayer as a means through which the people of God could help each other. The help that comes through prayer, however, is divine help in the form of deliverance from affliction, burden, and despair. Prayer is a means through which divine favors are bestowed upon God's people.

Ephesians 1:15-17: Here is Paul in Ephesians 1: 'For this reason I too, having heard of the faith in the Lord Jesus which *exists* among you and your love for all the saints, do not cease giving thanks for you, while making mention *of you* in my prayers; that the God of our Lord Jesus Christ, the Father of glory, may give to you a spirit of wisdom and of revelation in the knowledge of

Him' (Eph. 1:15-17). Paul's prayer had this goal in mind, 'that the God of our Lord Jesus Christ, the Father of glory, may give to you a spirit of wisdom and of revelation in the knowledge of Him.' This clearly implies that our Father in heaven does something to elect and believing souls on the earth through prayer.

And finally, listen to Philippians 1:9-11:

> '9And this I pray, that your love may abound still more and more in real knowledge and all discernment, 10so that you may approve the things that are excellent, in order to be sincere and blameless until the day of Christ; 11having been filled with the fruit of righteousness which *comes* through Jesus Christ, to the glory and praise of God.'

It is obvious from the context that Paul is praying to God (1:3). In 1:9 he prays that God would change the souls of the Philippians. The goal (or content) of his prayer is that their 'love may abound still more and more in real knowledge and all discernment.' Paul was imprisoned in Rome while writing Philippians.[18] Most likely, he prayed while in prison to God in heaven for souls in Macedonia. He wanted souls changed. He wanted the grace of love to abound in others, so he prayed. This implies that prayer is a means whereby God changes souls on the earth, causing (in this case) the grace of love to grow.

Having examined Ephesians 3:16-17 in some detail and seeing there that prayer is a means of grace illumines other passages where Paul mentions prayer. Only four were mentioned above, but there are many others.[19] There is a rich theology of prayer in Paul's letters and the rest of the Bible. According to Paul, prayer is a means through which the Father sends grace procured by the

18. This is the case with Ephesians as well.

19. Understanding prayer as a means of grace, as I have argued above, also sheds theological light on Paul's opening salutations: 'Grace to you and peace from God our Father and the Lord Jesus Christ' (Eph. 1:2).

Son to the souls of men delivered by the Spirit. Paul views prayer as a means of grace in a trinitarian economy of redemption.

Ephesians 3:16-17 and the Lord's Supper

How does this relate to the Lord's Supper? Prayer is a means through which God does things to souls, when he pleases. It is a means of grace, though it does not work *ex opere operato*. God remains the sovereign granter who grants what is requested at his pleasure. At the Supper, the minister prays. He thanks God for the bread and the cup (1 Cor. 11:23-25) and asks his blessings upon the ordinance. In turn, the Spirit is a means through which that which is symbolized by the bread and cup – the benefits of Christ's death – is brought to the souls of believers (1 Cor. 10:16) by the blessing of God. The Spirit brings that which the Father has blessed us with in Christ and he does that through the means of grace as he pleases. Just as prayer does not work *ex opere operato*, neither does the Supper. Both the Lord's Supper and prayer are means of grace through which the Spirit of God brings soul-nourishing and faith-strengthening blessings from heaven to Christ's people on the earth by the blessing of God.

5

The Confessional and Catechetical Formulation of the Lord's Supper as a Means of Grace in the Reformed Creedal Tradition

The Reformed confessional and catechetical formulation of the doctrine of the Lord's Supper as a means of grace is not based on one biblical text or a few isolated proof texts. It is based upon a complex of texts, exegetical work upon those texts, the doctrines derived from those texts and others in concert with a redemptive-historical, whole-Bible awareness and in conversation with the history of the Christian theological tradition. The Reformed symbolic formulation of the Lord's Supper as a means of grace is based on at least the following inter-related biblical factors:

- The accounts in the Gospels of the institution of the Lord's Supper by Christ prior to his exaltation.
- The words of the apostle Paul in 1 Corinthians 10 and 11, which are inspired, post-ascension, explanatory applications of the doctrine of the Lord's Supper as instituted by Christ during his humiliation.

- The ministry of the Holy Spirit in relation to the exalted Redeemer in bringing mediatorial, redemptive benefits to the souls of believers through the use of means.
- Union with Christ through faith as a result of the work of the Holy Spirit.
- The grace of faith and how it grows and develops believers into Christ-likeness through the use of means.

We will look at the Reformed confessional formulation of the Lord's Supper as a means of grace then the catechetical documents. I view the Reformed catechisms as practical mechanisms through which the doctrines of the confessions were taught. Theological formulation came first (the confessions) and then practical reflection and instruction (the catechisms).

The exegetical and theological discussion in previous chapters focused on establishing from the Bible that and how the Lord's Supper is a means of grace. We will now examine Reformed confessions and catechisms to see how they have formulated this doctrine. As we work our way through these documents, I will comment where I think the confessions and catechisms illustrate the exegetical and theological discussion I have presented. This will display that my exegesis and theological formulation is not novel and, in fact, is in agreement with the Reformed view of the Supper as a means of grace. The purpose of this book is to show how the Lord's Supper is both a means of grace and more than a memory. I have sought to do that exegetically and theologically in preceding chapters. Now it is time to test my work with the voice of Reformed symbolic documents. Is that which was argued in previous chapters a novelty or does it comport with the voice of the church in ages past?

Reformed confessions on the Lord's Supper as a means of grace

In this section we will look at three confessions: The Belgic Confession of 1561 (a Continental Reformed product), The Westminster Confession of 1647 (a British Presbyterian product), and The Second London Confession of 1677/89 (a British Particular Baptist product). Though it is thought by some that the seventeenth-century Particular Baptists were bare memorialists, it will become obvious that this is not the case. It will become clear as well that, though each confession has its own nuances, there is substantial theological continuity between these creedal documents on the Lord's Supper as a means of grace.

The Belgic Confession (1561)

> We believe that our gracious God, on account of our weakness and infirmities, hath ordained the Sacraments for us, thereby to seal unto us his promises, and to be pledges of the good will and grace of God towards us, and also *to nourish and strengthen our faith,* which he hath joined to the word of the gospel, the better to present to our senses, both that which he signifies to us by his Word, and *that which he works inwardly in our hearts,* thereby assuring and confirming in us *the salvation which he imparts to us.* For they are *visible signs and seals of an inward and invisible thing,* by means where of *God worketh in us by the power of the Holy Ghost.* Therefore the signs are not in vain or insignificant, so as to deceive us. For *Jesus Christ is the true object presented by them,* without whom they would be of no moment.
>
> Moreover, we are satisfied with the number of Sacraments which Christ our Lord hath instituted, which are two only, namely, the Sacrament of Baptism, and the Holy Supper of our Lord Jesus Christ. (The Belgic Confession, Article XXXIII, 'Of the Sacraments'; emphasis added)[1]

1. All quotations of The Belgic Confession are from Philip Schaff, *The Creeds of*

The sacraments 'nourish and strengthen our faith.' God 'works inwardly in our hearts' and assures and confirms 'in us the salvation which he imparts to us.' The sacraments are 'visible signs and seals of an inward and invisible thing, by means whereof God worketh in us by the power of the Holy Ghost.' The sacraments are means of grace.

Article XXXV, 'Of the Holy Supper of our Lord Jesus Christ,' states:

> We believe and confess that our Saviour Jesus Christ did ordain and institute the Sacrament of the Holy Supper, *to nourish and support those whom he hath already regenerated and incorporated into his family* ... Jesus Christ ... *nourishes and strengthens the spiritual life of believers,* when they eat him, that is to say, when they apply and receive him *by faith, in the Spirit*.... [The sacrament of the Holy Supper is] for *the support of our spiritual life*. [The Holy Supper is] a spiritual table, at which *Christ communicates himself with all his benefits to us, and gives us there to enjoy both himself and the merits of his sufferings and death, nourishing, strengthening, and comforting* our poor comfortless souls, by the eating of his flesh, quickening and refreshing them by the drinking of his blood. (emphasis added)

The Holy Supper nourishes and supports 'those whom he hath already regenerated and incorporated into his family'. It is not a converting ordinance but a sanctifying one. At the Supper, Christ 'nourishes and strengthens the spiritual life of believers'. Christ is applied and received 'by faith' and 'in the Spirit'. The Holy Supper supports the spiritual life of believers. Christ 'communicates himself with all his benefits to us'. The Supper nourishes, strengthens, and comforts those who are regenerated and incorporated into Christ's family, the church. Again, the Supper is a means of grace and more than a memory.

Christendom with a History and Critical Notes: Volume III, The Evangelical Protestant Creeds (Grand Rapids: Baker Books, Reprinted 1996).

The Westminster Confession of Faith (1647)

The seventeenth-century Reformed confession produced by the Westminster Assembly, The Westminster Confession of Faith (WCF), says in its chapter 'Of Saving Faith':

> *The grace of faith,* whereby the elect are enabled to believe to the saving of their souls, is *the work of the Spirit of Christ in their hearts,* and is *ordinarily wrought by the ministry of the word:* by which also, and *by the administration of the sacraments, and prayer, it is increased and strengthened.* (WCF, XIV.1; emphasis added)[2]

This is the confession's concise statement on the concept of the means of grace. Saving faith is a grace-gift, the effect of the Spirit's work in the hearts of God's elect. It 'is ordinarily wrought' in the heart as a gift by the Spirit of Christ in conjunction with 'the ministry of the word' of God. Subsequent to the initial work of the Spirit in conjunction with the word, the word of God, 'the sacraments [i.e., baptism and the Lord's Supper], and prayer' are means through which saving faith 'is increased and strengthened.' Faith 'is increased and strengthened' through the Supper because it is a means of grace.

In paragraph 3 of the same chapter, the WCF says:

> This faith is *different in degrees, weak or strong;* may be often and many ways *assailed* and *weakened,* but gets the victory; *growing up* in many to the attainment of a full assurance through Christ, who is both the author and finisher of our faith. (WCF, XIV.3; emphasis added)

Saving faith, effected by the Spirit and wrought in the hearts of God's elect in conjunction with the word of God, 'is different in degrees.' It can be 'weak or strong' and 'may be often and many ways assailed and weakened.' It is clear in the context of this

---

2. All quotations of the WCF are taken from *Westminster Confession of Faith* (Glasgow: Free Presbyterian Publications, 1985, Fifth Reprint 1988).

chapter (and elsewhere in the confession) that the Lord's Supper is a means of grace which strengthens faith. The Lord's Supper is more than a memory.

In the WCF's chapter 'Of the Sacraments', we read:

> Sacraments are holy signs and seals of the covenant of grace, *immediately instituted by God, to represent Christ and his benefits, and to confirm our interest in him* ...' (WCF, XXVII.1; emphasis added)

> The *grace* which is exhibited in or by the sacraments, rightly used, is not conferred by any power in them; neither doth the efficacy of a sacrament depend upon the piety or intention of him that doth administer it, but *upon the work of the Spirit*, and the word of institution; which contains, together with a precept authorizing the use thereof, a promise of benefit to worthy receivers. (WCF, XXVII.3; emphasis added)

The sacraments are 'instituted by God to represent Christ and his benefits, and to confirm our interest in him.' 'The grace which is exhibited' is 'conferred ... upon the work of the Spirit.' The sacraments do not work *ex opere operato*. Grace is conferred 'upon the work of the Spirit.' The Sacraments are means of the grace of Christ due to the ministry of the Holy Spirit. The Supper is a means of grace.

In the chapter 'Of the Lord's Supper', we read:

> Our Lord Jesus, in the night wherein he was betrayed, instituted the sacrament of his body and blood, called the Lord's Supper, to be observed in his church unto the end of the world, *for the perpetual remembrance of the sacrifice of himself in his death, the sealing all benefits thereof unto true believers, their spiritual nourishment and growth in him*, their further engagement in and to all duties which they owe him, and *to be a bond and pledge of their communion with him*, and with each other, as members of his mystical body. (WCF, XXIX.1; emphasis added)

> *Worthy receivers,* outwardly partaking of the visible elements in this sacrament, *do then also inwardly by faith, really and indeed, yet not carnally and corporally, but spiritually, receive and feed upon Christ crucified, and all benefits of his death*: the body and blood of Christ being then not corporally or carnally in, with, or under the bread and wine; *but spiritually, present to the faith of believers in that ordinance,* as the elements themselves are to their outwards senses. (WCF, XXIX. 7; emphasis added)[3]

The Lord's Supper points us back to 'the sacrifice of himself'. It is a memorial of the death of Christ. It benefits 'true believers'. It causes 'spiritual growth and nourishment in him'. It is related to 'their communion with him'. It benefits 'worthy receivers' or believers alone. Believers 'inwardly by faith, really and indeed, yet not carnally and corporally, but spiritually, receive and feed upon Christ crucified, and all benefits of his death'. Christ's 'body and blood' are 'spiritually, present to the faith of believers in that ordinance'. The Supper is more than a memory.

The Second London Confession of 1677/89

The first paragraph of the 2nd LCF's chapter 'Of Saving Faith' is a slight revision of the WCF. It inserts 'baptism and the Lord's Supper' in place of 'the sacraments' and adds 'and other means appointed of God' after prayer and immediately prior to 'it is increased and strengthened'. The doctrine of the means of grace is the same as the WCF, though. Here is that paragraph:

> *The grace of faith,* whereby the elect are enabled to believe to the saving of their souls, is *the work of the Spirit of Christ in their hearts,* and is *ordinarily wrought by the ministry of the Word;* by which also, and *by the administration of baptism and the Lord's supper, prayer, and other means appointed of God, it is increased and strengthened.* (2nd LCF, 14:1; emphasis added)

3. *The Savoy Declaration* of 1658 is nearly word-for-word the same as the WCF at this point.

Faith is a gift, 'the work of the Spirit of Christ in' the hearts of God's elect. That initial work of the Spirit is subsequently 'increased and strengthened' 'by the administration of ... the Lord's supper.' The Supper increases and strengthens faith. It is a means of grace.

The third paragraph of chapter 14, 'Of Saving Faith', is longer in the 2nd LCF than the same paragraph in the WCF. The 2nd LCF follows The Savoy Declaration of 1658 at this point.[4] Here is the text:

> This faith, although it be *different in degrees,* and *may be weak or strong,* yet it is in the least degree of it different in the kind or nature of it, as is all other saving grace, from the faith and common grace of temporary believers; and therefore, though it *may be many times assailed and weakened,* yet it gets the victory, *growing up* in many to the attainment of a full assurance through Christ, who is both the author and finisher of our faith. (2nd LCF, 14:3; emphasis added)

Saving faith is 'different in degrees, and may be weak or strong', 'assailed and weakened'. The Lord's Supper is a means of grace, strengthening faith.

In the chapter, 'Of the Lord's Supper', the Particular Baptist 2nd LCF reads:

> The supper of the Lord Jesus was instituted by him the same night wherein he was betrayed, to be observed in his churches to the end of the world, *for the perpetual remembrance,* and shewing forth the sacrifice in his death, *confirmation of the faith of believers in all the benefits thereof, their spiritual nourishment and growth in him,* their further engagement in, and to all duties which they owe to him; and *to be a bond and pledge of their communion with him,* and with each other. (2nd LCF, 30:1; emphasis added)

4. Cf. Renihan, *True Confessions,* 120 for the text of 2nd LCF 14:1 side by side with the Savoy and WCF.

The Lord's Supper is a memorial, a 'remembrance' of Christ's death. It is a 'confirmation of the faith of believers in all the benefits [of the death of Christ]'. The Supper is a means through which believers receive 'spiritual nourishment and growth in him.' It is 'to be a bond and pledge of their communion with him'. The Supper is a means through which 'spiritual nourishment and growth in' Christ occurs. Something happens through the Supper that alters the souls of believers for the better. This is means of grace language. The Supper is more than a memory.

In 30:7 of the 2nd LCF, we read:

> *Worthy receivers*, outwardly partaking of the visible elements in this ordinance, do then also *inwardly by faith, really and indeed*, yet not carnally and corporally, but *spiritually receive, and feed upon Christ crucified, and all the benefits of his death*; the body and blood of Christ being then not corporally or carnally, but *spiritually present to the faith of believers* in that ordinance, as the elements themselves are to their outward senses. (2nd LCF, 30:7; emphasis added)

'Worthy receivers ... inwardly by faith ... spiritually receive, and feed upon Christ crucified, and all the benefits of his death' through the Supper. The Supper benefits believers alone. Christ is 'spiritually present to the faith of believers'. There is a spiritual transaction that takes place through the Supper. Believers 'spiritually receive, and feed upon Christ'. The body and blood of Christ are 'spiritually present to the faith of believers'. The Supper is more than a memory.

The confessions cited above are one and the same in terms of advocating the Lord's Supper as a means of grace. The exegetical and theological work in the previous chapters helps us understand what the confessions mean by their doctrinal formulations. The confessional formulations, as noted above, are based upon a complex of texts, exegetical work upon those texts, and the doctrines derived from those texts in concert with a whole-Bible awareness and in conversation with the history of the Christian theological tradition. The Reformed doctrine of the Lord's Supper as a means of grace and more than a memory is clearly contained in its confessional documents – Continental and British, Paedobaptist and Particular Baptist.

Reformed catechisms on the Lord's Supper as a means of grace

In this section we will look at four catechisms: The Heidelberg Catechism of 1563 (a Continental Reformed product), The Westminster Shorter Catechism of 1648 (a British Presbyterian product), An Orthodox Catechism of 1680 (a British Particular Baptist product), and The Baptist Catechism of 1693 (another British Particular Baptist product). We will study the Heidelberg and Orthodox Catechism and then the Shorter Catechism and the Baptist Catechism. The Orthodox Catechism is a Baptist revision of the Heidelberg, and the Baptist Catechism is a revision of the Shorter Catechism. It is sometimes thought that the seventeenth-century English Particular Baptists were memorialists in their view of the Supper. This was shown not to be the case in the previous section. Analyzing these two Particular Baptist catechisms will prove further that, though they held that the Supper looked back to the death of Christ, the Lord's Supper was more than a memory in the minds of the authors of these catechisms. It will also become clear that, though each of the four catechisms has its own nuances, there is substantial continuity between these catechetical documents on the Lord's Supper as a means of grace, just as there was in the confessions analyzed above.

The Heidelberg Catechism and An Orthodox Catechism

The Heidelberg Catechism (HC) of 1563 contains a section entitled 'Of God the Holy Ghost'. Question 53 asks, 'What dost thou believe concerning the Holy Ghost?' The answer brings us into the doctrine of the Trinity and the work of the Spirit in the application of redemption. Here is the answer:

> First, that he is co-eternal God with the Father and the Son. Secondly, that he is also given unto me, makes me by a true faith partaker of Christ and all his benefits, comforts me, and shall abide with me forever.

This is important for our discussion. In the biblical section of this book, we saw Paul's theology of the Spirit in relation to Christ and his benefits in the application of redemption. Here Paul's thought (and the thought found elsewhere in Scripture) is put into catechetical form. It is the work of the Spirit to make God's elect partakers of Christ through faith and the recipients of all his benefits.

The Particular Baptist pastor Hercules Collins was the author of An Orthodox Catechism.[5] He was also a signatory of the 2nd LCF. The catechism was published in 1680. It is a slight revision of the HC. Collins' catechism contains the same question and answer cited above. This indicates that the theology of the Spirit in relation to Christ's benefits getting to the souls of the elect is one and the same in both catechisms. This should not surprise us. The Particular Baptist 2nd LCF at 8:8 (echoing the WCF) says:

> To all those for whom Christ has obtained eternal redemption, He does certainly and effectually apply and communicate the same, making intercession for them; uniting them to Himself by His Spirit, revealing to them, in and by the Word, the mystery of salvation, persuading them to believe and obey, governing their hearts by His Word and Spirit ... (2nd LCF, 8:8)

5. Cf. Renihan, *True Confessions*, 235.

The Spirit of God effects union between Christ and his people. The eternal redemption obtained by Christ gets applied to souls in union with him by his Spirit. The Holy Spirit is the divine bond between elect sinners and their Redeemer. The theology of the confession and these catechisms is the same. The Holy Spirit brings the benefits of Christ to souls on the earth.

Questions 65-68 of the HC cover 'Of the Holy Sacraments'. Collins' catechism has two very minor changes. Here is Question 65 and its answer:

> Q.65 Since, then, we are made partakers of Christ and all his benefits by faith only, whence comes this faith?
>
> A.65 The Holy Ghost works it in our hearts by the preaching of the holy Gospel, and confirms it by the use of the holy Sacraments.

Believers 'are made partakers of Christ and all his benefits by faith'. The Spirit works faith in our hearts 'by the preaching of the holy Gospel'. The same Spirit 'confirms' our faith 'by the use of the holy Sacraments [i.e., baptism and the Lord's Supper]'.

Questions 75-85 of the HC come under the heading 'Of the Holy Supper of the Lord'. Questions 75-82 deal with issues especially relevant to our discussion. Collins' catechism has very minor revisions of the HC in this section. I will quote only a few of the relevant sections and make brief comment.

Question 75 asks, 'How is it signified and sealed unto thee in the Holy Supper that thou dost partake of the one sacrifice of Christ on the cross and all his benefits?' In the answer to this question we are told that Christ 'with his crucified body and shed blood ... feeds and nourishes' the souls of believers 'to everlasting life'. This feeding is said to be as certain 'as I receive from the hand of the minister, and taste with my mouth, the bread and cup of the *Lord*, which are given me as certain tokens of the body and blood of Christ'. The Lord's Supper is a means of grace where

Christ gives himself to believers. A transaction takes place between Christ and his people, causing his benefits to be fed to and nourish souls on the earth.

Question 76 asks:

> Q.76 Why, then, doth Christ call the bread his body, and the cup his blood, or the New Testament in his blood; and St. Paul, the communion of the body and blood of Christ?
>
> A.76 Christ speaks thus not without great cause: namely, not only to teach us thereby that like as bread and wine sustain this temporal life, so also his crucified body and shed blood are the true meat and drink of our souls unto life eternal; but much more, by this visible sign and pledge to assure us that we are as really partakers of his true body and blood, *through the working of the Holy Ghost* ...

Communion of the body and blood of Christ is effected 'through the working of the Holy Ghost'.

Question 81 asks, 'Who are to come unto the table of the Lord?' The answer includes these words: 'Those ... who ... desire more and more to strengthen their faith ...' The Lord's Supper is a means through which the faith of believers is strengthened.

The Shorter Catechism and The Baptist Catechism

The Baptist Catechism (BC) is a revision of the Shorter Catechism (SC) with evidence of minor dependence upon the Larger Catechism as well. It was probably written by William Collins, the co-editor (with Nehemiah Coxe) of the 2nd LCF.[6] The revisions in the places we will note are slight and do not affect the theology. The BC replaces the term 'sacrament' with 'baptism' and 'the Lord's Supper' in SC.Q.88 and 91. In SC.Q.96, we are

6. Cf. Renihan, *True Confessions*, 193-94. Collins was a signatory of the 2nd LCF. Coxe died in 1688.

asked, 'What is the Lord's Supper?' The answer is 'The Lord's Supper is a sacrament ...' The BC gives this answer, 'The Lord's Supper is an ordinance of the New Testament instituted by Jesus Christ ...' The rest of the answer is the same in both catechisms, except one minor change where 'his' replaces 'Christ's'. One other minor revision occurs in SC.Q.97, where 'least' is replaced by 'lest'.[7] We should not make too much of the replacement of the word sacrament. Though the word was dropped, the concept is maintained and there is evidence outside the 2nd LCF and the BC that seventeenth-century Particular Baptists utilized the term sacrament in other published writings.[8]

SC.Q.88 asks, 'What are the outward means whereby Christ communicates to us the benefits of redemption?' Here is its answer:

> *The outward and ordinary means* whereby *Christ communicateth to us the benefits of redemption*, are his ordinances, especially the word, *sacraments* [baptism and the Lord's Supper], and prayer; all which are made effectual to the elect for salvation. (emphasis added)

'[T]he word, sacraments [i.e., baptism and the Lord's Supper], and prayer' are '[t]he outward and ordinary means' of grace'. Through the Lord's Supper, 'Christ communicateth to us the benefits of redemption.' The Lord's Supper is a means of grace and more than a memory.

SC.Q.91 asks, 'How do the sacraments become effectual means of salvation?' The catechism's answer is:

> The sacraments [i.e., baptism and the Lord's Supper] become effectual means of salvation, not from any virtue in them, or in him that doth administer them; but only *by the blessing of Christ*,

7. Cf. Renihan, *True Confessions*, 226.

8. Cf. Collins, *An Orthodox Catechism*, cited above and n. 5 in Chapter 1.

> *and the working of his Spirit in them that by faith receive them.* (emphasis added)

The Lord's Supper becomes an 'effectual means of salvation'. It does so 'by the blessing of Christ, and the working of the Spirit in those that by faith receive [it]'. The Lord's Supper does not work *ex opere operato*. It is blessed by Christ to the end that it may become an 'effectual means of salvation'. Christ blesses the Supper and the Holy Spirit works grace in the souls of believers.

SC.Q.96 asks, 'What is the Lord's Supper?' It gives this answer:

> The Lord's Supper is a sacrament, wherein, by giving and receiving bread and wine, according to Christ's appointment, his death is shewed forth; and the *worthy receivers are,* not after a corporal and carnal manner, but *by faith, made partakers of his body and blood, with all his benefits, to their spiritual nourishment, and growth in grace.* (emphasis added)

'Worthy receivers are ... by faith, made partakers of his body and blood, with all his benefits, to their spiritual nourishment, and growth in grace.' The Lord's Supper is a means through which 'spiritual nourishment, and growth in grace' occurs in the souls of believers. Communion with Christ takes place through the Supper. It is more than a memory.

Summary and Conclusion

According to the Reformed documents above, the sacrament of the Lord's Supper is a faith-nourishing, outward ordinance. Faith is nourished by the work of the Holy Spirit. The Spirit of Christ takes the benefits of Christ and brings them to elect and believing souls on the earth. Grace from Christ is worked in the soul through the Supper by the Spirit in accordance with the blessing of God and not *ex opere operato*.

Both the Reformed confessions and catechisms analyzed above

teach that the Lord's Supper is a means of grace and more than a memory. The exegetical and theological conclusions drawn in chapters 3 through 5 are clearly incorporated into these creedal formulations. If the exegetical and theological arguments from those chapters are cogent and reflect the mind of God as penned by Paul, then the Reformed creedal statements are accurate summaries of the Bible's teaching. If the arguments from those chapters are either not cogent or do not reflect the mind of God as penned by Paul, then the Reformed creedal statements are inaccurate summaries of the Bible's teaching. If the biblical argumentation provided is accurate, reflecting the sense God intended by the words, then the Reformed creedal statements are faithful to the teaching of Scripture. I will allow the reader to decide for himself which is the case.

6

Final Thoughts

In the first chapter of this study, it was noted that the specific focus of this book is to show *how* the Lord's Supper is a means of grace and, therefore, more than a memory. I have argued that the Lord's Supper is a means of grace because of what the Holy Spirit does in the souls of believers when local churches partake of it. The Spirit effects (or enhances) present communion between the exalted Redeemer and his pilgrim people on the earth. The Lord's Supper is a means of grace through which Christ is present by his divine nature and through which the Holy Spirit nourishes the souls of believers with the benefits wrought for us in Christ's human nature which is now glorified and in heaven at the right hand of the Father.[1]

1. According to Muller, this is the Reformed view of the spiritual presence of Christ. '... the Reformed view of Christ's presence in the Lord's Supper [is] ... a spiritual presence (*praesentia spiritualis*) according to which the body and blood of Christ, now in heaven, are mediated to believers by the power of the Spirit.' Cf. Muller, *Dictionary*, 268.

Review of method and conclusions

The method which brought me to the conclusions drawn started with a specific text of Scripture – 1 Corinthians 10:16. As stated above, this is quite possibly the most explicit text in the New Testament (certainly in Paul's letters) on the nature of the Lord's Supper as a means of grace. The text was set in its context and examined in that light. The conclusion was that communion of the blood and of the body of Christ refers to present communion with or participation in the present benefits of Christ wrought for us by his death. This conclusion was supported by various secondary sources and shown to be contained in the doctrinal formulations of various Reformed confessions and catechisms. A question surfaced as a result of our findings: How are the benefits of Christ brought to elect and believing souls on the earth through the Supper? The answer was found in Paul's letter to the Ephesians.

Ephesians 1:3 teaches that the God and Father of our Lord Jesus Christ has blessed believers through the ministry of the Holy Spirit who brings 'every spiritual blessing' to the souls of those chosen by God before the foundation of the world (Eph. 1:4) and redeemed by Christ's blood (Eph. 1:7). The Spirit brings the eschatological blessings procured by Christ to the souls of men. Believers taste of the world-to-come by the ministry of the Spirit due to their union with Christ. The Spirit's ministry through the Supper is the bond between the exalted Redeemer and his people on the earth. The Spirit is the One who works in us based on the fact of Christ's work for us. These are blessings received by believers from the Father. This understanding of Ephesians 1:3 was supported by secondary sources and seen in the doctrinal formulations of the Reformed creedal tradition.

Ephesians 3:16-17 was also examined. This text teaches clearly that prayer is a means through which our Father changes souls by the ministry of the Spirit. Spiritual invigoration that strengthens faith is a result of requesting blessing from heaven. The Spirit of the Father brings heavenly blessings procured by Christ to souls through prayer. Since prayer is offered during the Supper, our Father sends the Spirit in answer to prayer and he blesses the Supper producing further communion between the Redeemer and his people on earth. This understanding of Ephesians 3:16-17 was supported by secondary sources and the theology of this text was shown to have made its way into the doctrinal formulations of the Reformed tradition.

In Chapter 1, I stated the specific focus of this study as follows: 'My specific focus is to show you *how* the Lord's Supper is a means of grace.' I sought to do so upon the exegesis of pertinent biblical texts and the theological implications of those texts in relation to the Lord's Supper. My biblical and theological conclusions were shown to be reflected in the Reformed tradition's creedal statements on the Lord's Supper as a means of grace. I will let my case stand as is and complete this study with some theological musings and practical and pastoral implications in light of the discussion.

Theological musings on the Supper as a means of grace

There are many theological issues connected to the Lord's Supper that have been discussed above and many more that could have been. I will now mention three issues of importance related to the discussion above.

The theology of the Lord's Supper as a means of grace advocated above is clearly trinitarian.

The Father blesses believers through the Supper based on the Son's work for them which is the ground upon which the Spirit works in them. The Father elects and predestinates. The Son redeems. The

Father and the Son send the Spirit (John 14:26; 15:26; 16:7; Acts 2:33 [Luke 24:49]; Eph. 1:3), who brings the fruits of redemption to the souls of men. That which the Father sent the Son to procure for us is brought to us through means by the blessing of God through prayer. The Spirit is the divine deliverer of the benefits wrought by the incarnate Son of God through the means of grace. The Father blesses by sending the Son to procure redemption and all its benefits and by sending the Spirit to apply those benefits. This view of the Supper ought to remind us that Christianity is a robustly trinitarian religion.

THIS VIEW OF THE SUPPER ALSO HIGHLIGHTS 'A ROBUSTLY PNEUMATOLOGICAL UNDERSTANDING OF THE SACRAMENT'.[2] Understanding the role of the Spirit is vital in order to understand the Supper as a means of grace.[3] As Horton asserts, 'The communion ... derives its efficacy only through the powerful working of the Holy Spirit.'[4] In one sense, the theological key that unlocks the door to understand how the Supper is a means of grace is the doctrine of the work of the Spirit (within its trinitarian context) and how he uses means to deliver the benefits of redemption to us. And we should remind ourselves that the benefits of redemption include the whole Redeemer. The Spirit brings Christ to the souls of believers through means. In the words of Ferguson, 'In the Supper ... we commune with the person of Christ in the mystery of the hypostatic union; we do so *S/spiritually, i.e.* through the power of the Spirit.'[5] Through the means of grace the Spirit of God strengthens the faith of the

2. Horton, *The Christian Faith*, 810.
3. Cf. Ferguson, *The Holy Spirit*, 201, where he says, '... the role of the Spirit is so vital in the Supper.'
4. Michael Horton, *A Better Way: Rediscovering the Drama of Christ-Centered Worship* (Grand Rapids: Baker Books, 2002, Paperback edition published 2003), 120.
5. Ferguson, *The Holy Spirit*, 203.

people of God so that the Christ of God may dwell in them. This happens through the Supper by the blessing of God.

This view of the Supper assumes and demands the primacy of the written word of God as the chief means of grace. That the word of God is a means of grace is clear from 1 Peter 2:2, Acts 20:32, John 17:17, Jude 20, and Ephesians 4:15.[6] It is a means whereby we grow, are built up, sanctified, and grow up into Christ. Though the Lord's Supper was instituted by the spoken word of the incarnate Son of God, it is the written word of God that explains its meaning to us (and, as I have argued, Paul is the chief theologian of the Supper in the New Testament). The Lord's Supper is not a stand-alone ordinance. It does not preach itself. It needs to be explained. Its efficacy is vitally dependent upon the written word of God. The Spirit of God takes the data of the written word of God which centers on the glorious, incarnate Son of God and brings it to the people of God. The word should be preached to set up the Supper.

Practical and pastoral implications

As a pastor, thinking through these issues forced me to ask some questions and try to work through some implications. I do not claim to have all the answers but think it would be good to work through some of these questions and implications together.

If the Lord's Supper is a means of grace wherein the Holy Spirit brings to the souls of believers the benefits of Christ's body and blood, then it is more than a memory.

Davis says, '... [In] the New Testament period, in the celebration of the Lord's Supper "... there is no intimation that

6. Notice here that it is not people that are means but truth spoken.

this meal was to be only a reminder of either a past event or an absent loved one.'"[7] Though it is a reminder of a past event, it is more than that. Through the Supper, because it is a means of grace, purchased grace, redemptive grace, sanctifying grace is ushered into souls, special delivery, from our exalted Redeemer by the power of the Holy Spirit. John Willison captures the doctrine well, saying:

> Though Christ is not bodily present, yet he is really and truly present in a spiritual and invisible manner. He is present by his God-head, and by his Spirit. He is present by his power and efficacy, communicating and applying the virtue of his death: and thus we are really made partakers of Christ in this ordinance. We partake of the sun when we have its beams of light and heart [*sic*; 'heat'?] darted down upon us, although we have not the bulk and body of the sun put into our hands: so we partake of Christ in the sacrament, when we share his grace, and the blessed fruits of his broken body, though we do not actually eat his flesh with our mouths.[8]

The Supper is more than a memory. It is a means through which Christ comes to souls. "The Lord's Supper is an occasion when the Lord Jesus feeds the souls of his people, thus making the meal a means of grace."[9] The people of God need to know this and be reminded of it often.

If the Lord's Supper is a means of grace through which the Holy Spirit brings to the souls of believers the benefits of Christ's body and blood and, as a result, souls are nourished, then we ought to think seriously about the corporate attitude or climate during the Supper. Should the Supper be a celebration? Should there be joy in our hearts while partaking? Should the Supper be like a funeral

7. Davis, *Worship and the Reality of God*, 116. Davis is quoting Martin J. Heinecken.

8. Quoted in Maclean, *The Lord's Supper*, 104.

9. Maclean, *The Lord's Supper*, 172.

procession for an absent loved one?[10] Should the Supper be more like a Protestant confessional than an occasion for joy and hope? Should we tell our people to bow their heads in shame, confessing their sins, and if they don't feel bad enough forbid them from partaking or encourage them not to partake? Or maybe the Supper should be looked upon as a reward for a good week, assuming one passes the test of self-examination? I am thinking here of the misuse of 1 Corinthians 11:28: 'But a man must examine himself, and in so doing he is to eat of the bread and drink of the cup.' The context indicates that the primary focus of this examination concerns horizontal divisions in the church (1 Cor. 11:17ff.).[11] We must keep short accounts with fellow church members. Also, it seems to me that the self-examination should take place prior to coming to the Supper, not at the communion service.[12] This way there is time to remedy any problems between church members (or in our own souls). The way Paul states it gives the impression that he expected the self-examination to result in taking the Supper. Maclean agrees:

> Paul does not expect self-examination to result in a person not partaking. His comment is, 'Let a man examine himself, *and so let him eat*' (11:28). This expectation is noteworthy given the lax procedures tolerated in Corinth. Paul anticipated that 'any unworthy Christian would make the necessary amendments immediately'.[13]

---

10. Some of these questions come from others whom I have read.

11. It could go back further to include the issue of Christian liberty and idolatry as well. Commenting on 1 Corinthians 11:28-29, Horton says, 'The context, however, is all-important, as the warning is couched in a disciplinary argument against idolatry and schism.' Cf. Horton, *God of Promise*, 157-58 for further discussion.

12. This is the view of the Westminster Larger Catechism, Q. 171.

13. Maclean, *The Lord's Supper*, 38. Maclean is quoting Donald Macleod, 'Qualifications for Communion' in *Banner of Truth*, No. 65, 17. Obviously, if the necessary amendments are not made, the person should not partake.

In my experience, this verse is often used for individuals to examine, for instance, how many times they read their Bible or how long and fervent their prayers were in the recent past. If they fail the test, a form of self-excommunication is enacted and the Supper is not taken. For some, this may even be viewed as an act of piety and reverence. Though we ought to read our Bibles and pray privately, I do not think that is what Paul had in mind. I rather think that since no one reads their Bibles and prays perfectly, instead of being an argument not to take the Supper it is just the opposite. I agree with Horton, when he says, "The Supper is a means of grace for the weak, not a reward for the strong."[14] Because it is a means of grace for believing sinners, though seriousness and reverence and awe are certainly appropriate, joy[15] and hope ought to have their place as well because we are feasting upon Christ, further tasting that the Lord is good, and being helped along as pilgrims in a foreign land.

We should be very careful how we fence the table.[16] Under normal circumstances, the only church members under our charge who should be forbidden to partake are those under formal church discipline. For all others, it is a means of grace for weak souls which need to be strengthened. Just as we would never tell believers to stop reading their Bibles because they had a bad week or stop praying because they are not holy enough or feel unworthy, we should not forbid the Supper under normal circumstances. The Supper is a joy- and hope-inducing ordinance. It gives us renewed confidence that our sins are forgiven, that Christ is ours and we are his, and an expectation of more of Christ to come.

---

14. Horton, *The Christian Faith*, 819.

15. Remember, 'joy' is a fruit of the Spirit (Gal. 5:22).

16. Cf. Maclean, *The Lord's Supper*, 152. The unbaptized should be told that the Supper is not for them. The church member in good standing should be assured that the Supper is for them, assuming any necessary amendments in light of 1 Cor. 11:28 have been made.

IF THE LORD'S SUPPER IS A MEANS OF GRACE THROUGH WHICH THE HOLY SPIRIT BRINGS TO THE SOULS OF BELIEVERS THE BENEFITS OF CHRIST'S BODY AND BLOOD AND, AS A RESULT, SOULS ARE NOURISHED, THEN WE OUGHT TO THINK SERIOUSLY ABOUT ITS FREQUENCY.

The frequency of the Supper is also a question worth pursuing in light of our study. The Supper is a sacred, covenantal meal. It is a means of grace. But how often should churches take the Supper? Some are re-thinking this issue in our day and are celebrating communion more frequently than in the past. Others, out of concern not to trivialize the sacred (a concern I share), are content with a monthly or less-frequent celebration. But prayer is sacred, and the reading and preaching of the word are sacred, and no one (as far as I know) argues from that to less frequent public prayer and less frequent public reading and preaching of the word of God. These words by John Brown of Haddington make this point well.

> ... I fear it will be no easy task to prove that our way of administering the Supper is agreeable to the Word of God.... That its infrequency tends to make it solemn I do not see, for if it so why not administer baptism but once a year also, as it, in its own nature, is as solemn as the Supper? Why not pray seldom, preach seldom, read God's Word seldom, that they may become more solemn too?[17]

Horton suggests that a diminished interest in frequent communion is the product of an inordinate emphasis upon 'the individual's inner piety'. He says:

> The problem with the pietistic version of the Lord's Supper, therefore, is that in its obsession with the individual's inner piety, it loses much of the import of the feast as a sacred meal that actually binds us to Christ and to each other. Instead of viewing it first as God's saving action toward us and then our fellowship with each other in Christ, we come to see it as just another opportunity to

17. Cited in Maclean, *The Lord's Supper*, 235.

> be threatened with the law. Instead of celebrating the foretaste of the marriage supper of the Lamb on Mount Zion, we are still trembling at the foot of Mount Sinai. It is no wonder, then, that there is a diminished interest in frequent communion.[18]

Whether Horton is right or not, I do not think the trivializing of the sacred by a too frequent celebration of the Supper argument is valid.

It is clear that the New Testament nowhere commands weekly communion, but neither does it command weekly singing or weekly prayer or weekly preaching, at least not explicitly. We believe in weekly corporate singing (and prayer and preaching) by the church because we believe it is necessarily contained in the Holy Scripture, and rightly so.[19] Singing is an element of public worship and is a means of grace of a sort but only if and when we sing the truths of the word of God. Singing can be conducted more than once, and it ought to be done at least on the Lord's Day when the church gathers. But we also believe that the Supper is an element of public worship and repeatable, unlike baptism (though we can be reminded of our baptism), and ought to be conducted on the Lord's Day, at least ordinarily. But how many Lord's Days per year? How many Lord's Days per month? These are questions pastors and churches must wrestle with.

The early church apparently celebrated the Supper weekly. *The Didache* 14:1 says, 'On the Lord's own day gather together and break bread and give thanks.'[20] It appears that the Supper

---

18. Horton, *God of Promise*, 160-61.

19. Cf. Ryan M. McGraw, *By Good and Necessary Consequence* (Grand Rapids: Reformation Heritage Books, 2012) for a very helpful discussion on the biblical, theological, and historical issues related to WCF I.6, 'by good and necessary consequence may be deduced from Scripture.' He suggests that 'necessarily contained in Scripture' (2nd LCF 1:6) and 'by good and necessary consequence may be deduced from Scripture' are functionally equivalent.

20. Holmes, *The Apostolic Fathers*, 365. Interestingly, the Greek text reads Κατὰ

was so important to the early church that the early believers took it weekly.[21] It could be that they made a theological connection between a weekly Lord's Day and a weekly Lord's Supper.[22] Whatever the case, it is important to think through the issue of frequency with the fact that the Lord's Supper, like the word of God and prayer, is a means of grace.

The Lord's Supper has links with the past, the present and the future and we need to make sure we are highlighting each when we take the Supper.

The Supper is clearly linked with the past – 'Do this in remembrance of me' (1 Cor. 11:24-25). The Lord's Supper is also linked to the present – 'The cup of blessing which we bless, is it not the communion of the blood of Christ? The bread which we break, is it not the communion of the body of Christ?' (1 Cor. 10:16). But the New Testament also links the Supper with the future – 'For as often as you eat this bread and drink this cup, you proclaim the Lord's death till He comes' (1 Cor. 11:29) and 'But I say to you, I will not drink of this fruit of the vine from now on until that day when I drink it new with you in My Father's kingdom' (Matt. 26:29 [cf. Rev. 19:7-9]).

These connections with the *past*, the *present*, and the *future* (i.e., the three tenses of the Lord's Supper) provide conceptual links between the Lord's Supper and the Lord's Day. Like the Lord's Supper the Lord's Day looks back to redemption accomplished –

κυριακὴν δὲ κυρίου (literally, 'And according to the Lord's of the Lord'). Κυριακὴν ('the Lord's') is the same word (an adjective) used in 1 Corinthians 11:20 of the Lord's Supper and Revelation 1:10 of the Lord's Day. Holmes' translation assumes an ellipsis, supplying 'day' to complete the thought. It appears that *The Didache* is connecting the Lord's Day with the Lord's Supper.

21. Maclean says weekly communion was the practice of the church until the fifth century. Cf. Maclean, *The Lord's Supper*, 101.

22. See below.

the Lord's Supper looking back to Christ's death and the Lord's Day to his resurrection. Like the Lord's Supper the Lord's Day is a celebration of redemption historically accomplished and presently applied. And like the Lord's Supper the Lord's Day is a down-payment of the future, a pledge of the age-to-come. Christ's resurrection on the first Lord's Day inaugurated the overlapping of the ages and since we commune with our Lord Jesus who is in heaven in his age-to-come glorified humanity and further receive age-to-come blessings through the Supper by the ministry of the Holy Spirit, the Lord's Supper, like the Lord's Day, is a pledge of more glory to come.

Finis

I will close with the words of William Kiffin, a leading seventeenth-century English Particular Baptist. Steve Weaver says:

> While arguing for the priority of baptism before the Lord's Supper in the life of the believer, Kiffin describes baptism as 'the Sacrament of Spiritual *Birth*' and the Lord's Supper as the sacrament of 'Spiritual *Nourishment* or *Growth*' by which believers are *Spiritually fed*.[23]

May we come to a new (if needed) and/or fresh appreciation for and experience of Christ through the Supper which is a means of grace and more than a memory.

23. Cited in Steve Weaver's unpublished *Christ Spiritually Present and Believers Spiritually Nourished*, 18-19. Weaver is quoting William Kiffin, *A Sober Discourse of Right to Church-Communion* (London: Geo. Larkin, 1681), 23.

Bibliography

Arnold, Clinton E. *Exegetical Commentary on the New Testament: Ephesians*. Grand Rapids: Zondervan, 2010.

The Baptist Confession of Faith & The Baptist Catechism. Vestavia Hills, AL: Solid Ground Christian Books and Carlisle, PA: Reformed Baptist Publications, 2010.

Barcellos, Richard C. 'The New Testament Theology of the Sabbath: Christ, the Change of the Day and the Name of the Day' in *Reformed Baptist Theological Review* V:1 (Spring 2008).

Bavinck, Herman. *Reformed Dogmatics: Holy Spirit, Church, and New Creation*, IV, translated by John Vriend. Grand Rapids: Baker Academic, 2008.

Bauer, Walter. Revised and Edited by Frederick William Danker, Third Edition. *A Greek-English Lexicon of the New Testament and Other Early Christian Literature*. Chicago: The University of Chicago Press, 2000.

Beale, G. K. and Carson, D. A., Editors. *Commentary on the New Testament Use of the Old Testament.* Grand Rapids: Baker Academic, 2007.

Beddome, Benjamin. *A Scriptural Exposition of the Baptist Catechism.* Vestavia Hills, AL: Solid Ground Christian Books, 2006.

Berkhof, Louis. *Systematic Theology.* Grand Rapids: William. B. Eerdmans Publishing Company, 1938, Reprinted 1986.

Bernard, Thomas Dehany. *The Progress of Doctrine in the New Testament.* New York: American Tract Society, n.d.

Brown, Colin, Editor. *The New International Dictionary of New Testament Theology,* Volumes 1 and 2. Grand Rapids: Zondervan Publishing House, 1986.

Calvin, John. *Institutes of the Christian Religion.* Philadelphia: The Westminster Press, 1960.

Davis, John Jefferson. *Worship and the Reality of God: An Evangelical Theology of Real Presence.* Downers Grove, IL: InterVarsity Press, 2010.

Eadie, John. *Ephesians.* Minneapolis: James & Klock Christian Publishing Company, 1883, Reprinted 1977.

Ferguson, Sinclair B. *The Holy Spirit.* Downers Grove, IL: InterVarsity Press, 1996.

Gaebelein, Frank E., Editor. *The Expositor's Bible Commentary, Volume I.* Grand Rapids: Zondervan Publishing House, 1979.

George, Timothy. *Theology of the Reformers.* Nashville, TN: Broadman Press, 1988.

Gill, John. *Exposition of the Old and New Testaments*, Volume 8. Paris, AR: The Baptist Standard Bearer, Inc., 1810, Reprinted 1989.

Graham, Glenn H. *An Exegetical Summary of Ephesians*, Second Edition 2008. Dallas: SIL International, 1997.

Haykin, Michael A. G. *Kiffin, Knollys and Keach: Rediscovering our English Baptist heritage.* Leeds, England: Reformation Today Trust, 1996.

Hodge, Charles. *A Commentary on 1&2 Corinthians*. Edinburgh, Scotland and Carlisle, PA: The Banner of Truth Trust, 1857, Reprinted 1983.

______________. *A Commentary on the Epistle to the Ephesians*. New York: Hodder & Stoughton, 1856.

Hoehner, Harold W. *Ephesians: An Exegetical Commentary*. Grand Rapids: Baker Academic, 2002.

Holmes, Michael W., Editor and Translator. *The Apostolic Fathers: Greek Texts and English Translations,* third edition. Grand Rapids: Baker Academic, 2007.

Horton, Michael. *A Better Way: Rediscovering the Drama of God-Centered Worship*. Grand Rapids: Baker Books, 2002, Paperback edition published 2003.

______________. *God of Promise: Introducing Covenant Theology*. Grand Rapids: Baker Books, 2006.

______________. *The Christian Faith: A Systematic Theology for Pilgrims on the Way*. Grand Rapids: Zondervan, 2011.

Hyde, Daniel R. *In Living Color: Images of Christ and the Means of Grace*. Grandville, MI: Reformed Fellowship, Inc., 2009.

Johnson, Edna. *A Semantic Structural Analysis of Ephesians*. Dallas: SIL International, 2008.

Larkin, William J. *Ephesians: A Handbook on the Greek Text*. Waco, TX: Baylor University Press, 2009.

Letham, Robert. *The Lord's Supper: Eternal Word in Broken Bread*. Phillipsburg, NJ: P&R Publishing, 2001.

Lincoln, Andrew T. *Word Biblical Commentary, Volume 42, Ephesians*. Dallas: Word Books, Publisher, 1990.

Maclean, Malcolm. *The Lord's Supper*. Fearn, Ross-shire, Scotland: Christian Focus Publications, 2009.

Mathison, Keith A. *Given For You: Reclaiming Calvin's Doctrine of the Lord's Supper*. Phillipsburg, NJ: P&R Publishing, 2002.

McGraw, Ryan M. *By Good and Necessary Consequence*. Grand Rapids: Reformation Heritage Books, 2012.

Muller, Richard A. *Dictionary of Latin and Greek Theological Terms*. Grand Rapids: Baker Book House, 1985, Second printing, September 1986.

O'Brien, Peter T. *The Letter to the Ephesians*, Pillar New Testament Commentary. Grand Rapids: William B. Eerdmans Publishing Company, 1999.

Olinger, Danny E., Editor. *A Geerhardus Vos Anthology: Biblical and Theological Insights Alphabetically Arranged*. Phillipsburg, NJ: P&R Publishing, 2005.

Payne, Jon D. *John Owen on the Lord's Supper*. Edinburgh, Scotland and Carlisle, PA: The Banner of Truth Trust, 2004.

Phillips, Richard D. *What is the Lord's Supper?* Phillipsburg, NJ: P&R Publishing, 2005.

Renihan, James M. *Edification and Beauty: The Practical Ecclesiology of the English Particular Baptists, 1675-1705*. Eugene, OR: Wipf & Stock Publishers, 2008.

______________, Editor. *True Confessions: Baptist Documents in the Reformed Family*. Owensboro, KY: RBAP, 2004.

Schaff, Philip. *The Creeds of Christendom with a History and Critical Notes: Volume III, The Evangelical Protestant Creeds*. Grand Rapids: Baker Books, Reprinted 1996.

Thielman, Frank. *Ephesians*, Baker Exegetical Commentary on the New Testament. Grand Rapids: Baker Academic, 2010.

Thiselton, Anthony C. *The First Epistle to the Corinthians: A Commentary on the Greek Text*. Grand Rapids: William B. Eerdmans Publishing Company, 2000.

Vanhoozer, Kevin J., General Editor. *Dictionary for Theological Interpretation of the Bible*. Grand Rapids: Baker Academic, 2005.

Vos, Geerhardus. *The Pauline Eschatology*. Phillipsburg, NJ: P&R Publishing, 1930, Reprinted 1991.

Wallace, Daniel B. *Greek Grammar Beyond the Basics: An Exegetical Syntax of the New Testament*. Grand Rapids: Zondervan, 1996.

Weaver, Steve. *Christ Spiritually Present and Believers Spiritually Nourished: The Lord's Supper in Seventeenth-Century Particular Baptist Life*. Unpublished.

Westminster Confession of Faith. Glasgow: Free Presbyterian Publications, 1985, Fifth Reprint 1988.

Wilson, Geoffrey B. *1 Corinthians: A Digest of Reformed Comment.* Edinburgh, Scotland and Carlisle, PA: The Banner of Truth Trust, 1978.

Name and Subject Index

Aa

Adam ... 63, 69

Arnold, Clinton E. ... 61

Bb

baptism ... 93-4, 100, 112, 114

Baptist Catechism (1693) ... 96, 99-100

Barcellos, Richard C. ... 35n

Bavinck, Herman ... 23, 54, 70

Bauer, Walter ... 46

Beale, G. K. ... 44

Beddome, Benjamin ... 24n

Belgic Confession (1561) ... 89-90

Berkhof, Louis ... 41

Bernard, Thomas D. ... 17

Bible study ... 28-9, 110

Bietenhard, H. ... 51-62

Blaiklock, Edward M. ... 17

blessing of God ... 59-62, 64-5, 66-7

... 69-70, 104

blood of Christ ... 33-4, 42, 45, 48-50

... 52-3, 69-70, 92-3, 99, 113

body of Christ ... 33-4, 42, 45, 48-50

... 52-63, 69-70, 92-3, 99, 113

breaking of bread ... 33, 42

Brown, John ... 111

Cc

Calvin, John ... 16, 27

Carson, D. A. ... 44

catechisms ... 96-101

Cephas ... 80

Ciampa, Roy E. ... 43-4

Collins, Hercules ... 24n, 97, 98

Collins, William ... 99

communion

- and fellowship with Christ ... 53-54
- frequency of ... 111-2
- and 'koinonia' ... 45-7, 49

and memorial aspect of Lord's Supper 25-6

present..................28, 37-8, 48-9, 52, 103-4

and sharing..34

and Spirit of God................................106-7

complexity of subject..................................26-7

confessional Reformed churches....21, 21n, 28 87-8

covenant of redemption..............................58-9

covenantal meals................................. 35-7, 111

cup of the Lord...........................34, 42, 51, 113

Dd

Davis, John Jefferson.......................... 47, 107-8

Day of the Lord................................ 35, 113-4

'demons'...51-2

doctrinal formulation of the Lord's Supper

Belgic Confession................................89-90

catechisms.. 96-101

and confessional Reformed churches...87-8

Second London Confession of Faith ...21-2 93-6

Westminster Confession of Faith.........91-3

Ee

Eadie, John....................... 60, 62, 66, 68, 78, 79

eschatological anticipation of Lord's Supper 37-9, 113

Eucharist..32, 32n, 50

Ff

faith.................................... 88-95, 97-9, 101-2

fellowship with Christ..............................53-4

Ferguson, Sinclair 70, 106

focus of study 28, 103

food at Lord's Supper....................................34

frequency of Supper celebrations............111-3

Gg

Gaebelein, Franke E...18

Garland, David E. 42-53

General Assembly of the Association of Reformed Baptist Churches of America......15

George, Timothy...25

Gill, John...52

Graham, Glenn H......................... 75, 76n, 82n

God

blessing of.....59-62, 64-5, 66-7, 69-70, 104

and covenantal meals 35-7

and 'means of grace' .... 23-4, 70, 85 .... 104-5, 107

and Paul's prayer...............................77-9, 82

praise for..............59-60, 62, 64-5, 64-7, 71

and prayer 83-5, 104-5

and redemption 55-6

Spirit of......................................65-6, 106-7

triune nature................. 55-6, 58-62, 105-6

Word of... 24, 107

grace

and doctrinal formulation of the Lord's Supper...87-94

means of..................15-16, 22-4, 27-8, 41-2 ....52-3, 70, 85, 103-7

and prayer 73-4, 77, 82-5, 104-5

Hh

Haykin, Michael A. G. 24

heavenly realm..67-8

Heidelberg Catechism (1563)...................96-9

Hodge, Charles... 53, 67

Hoehner, Harold W.....................................56-7

Holmes, Michael W...............32n, 112n, 113n

Holy Spirit

and blessings of God....................69-70, 104
and catechisms..97-8
and heavenly realm..................................67-8
and mediation of Christ.......................69-71
and prayer 74, 79-82
and redemption 54, 55, 70, 73
as Spirit of God..........................65-6, 106-7
and spiritual nourishment................ 28, 103
Horton, Michael 36-7, 106, 110, 111-2
Hyde, Daniel R. 24n

Ii

idolatry...42-5, 50-2
Institutes of the Christian Religion (book)......16
Israel........................... 35-6, 43-4, 50-1, 63, 69

Jj

Jesus Christ
ascension of..35
and blessings of God...................69-70, 104
blood of....33-4, 42, 45, 48-50, 52-3, 69-70
....92-3, 99, 113
body of......33-4, 42, 45, 48-50, 52-3, 69-70
....92-3, 99, 113
and breaking of bread 33, 42
and catechisms.................................. 97-101
and covenantal meals 36
cup of.....................................34, 42, 51, 113
Day of... 35, 113-4
death of........................ 25, 33, 37, 39, 85, 93
....95, 104, 114
doctrinal formulation of the Lord's Supper 21-2, 88-95
and eschatological anticipation of Lord's Supper...37-8
fellowship with 53-4
food of...34-5
indwelling of..80-91
and 'koinonia'.....................................45-8, 53
and 'means of grace'......... 23-4, 28, 52-3, 70
....85,103-4
as mediator..69-71
and memorial aspect of Lord's Supper 25-6, 37, 95, 107-8
obedience of... 63, 69
and Paul's prayer...................................79-83
and prayer 83-5
and redemption 18, 37, 54, 58-9, 70, 100
resurrection of 18, 114
and salvation 59
solidarity in 68-9
table of.. 34, 51-2, 99
and thankfulness 31-43
union with................................. 68-9, 88, 98
Johnson, Edna 61
joy 108, 110

Kk

Käsemann, Ernst..47-8
Keach, Benjamin 52
Kiffin, William 114
'koinonia'....................................45-50, 46n, 53

Ll

Larkin, William J...............................61-2, 62-3
Letham, Robert...................25n, 31n, 33n, 41n
Lincoln, Andrew T...............................67, 80-1
Luther, Martin...26

Mm

Maclean, Malcolm.................................. 53, 109
Mathison, Keith A.....25n, 26n, 31n, 41n, 45n

McGraw, Ryan M. ... 112n
memorial aspect of Lord's Supper ... 22-3, 25-7
... 37, 95, 101-2, 107-8
method of study ... 28-9, 104
Moses ... 35-6
Muller, Richard A. ... 24n, 58n, 59n, 103n

Nn

nature of Lord's Supper ... 42, 45-8, 53
New International Dictionary of New Testament Theology ... 49
New Testament terminology ... 31-9

Oo

O'Brien, Peter T. ... 62, 64, 67-8
Olinger, Danny E. ... 38n, 39n
ordinances ... 24-5, 24n
Orthodox Catechism (1680) ... 96, 97-9

Pp

pagan sacrificial meals ... 44-5, 50-2
participation ... 44-7, 49
pastoral implications ... 107-14
Paul
  and blessing of God ... 59-62, 64-5, 66-7
  and breaking of bread ... 33, 42
  and catechisms ... 97
  and doctrinal formulation of the Lord's Supper ... 87
  and eschatological anticipation of Lord's Supper ... 38
  and idolatry ... 42-5, 50-2
  imprisoned in Rome ... 84
  and 'koinonia' ... 45, 46-9
  and nature of Lord's Supper ... 42, 45-8, 53
  praise for God ... 59-60, 62, 64-5, 66-7
  and prayer ... 82-5
  prayer of ... 74-82
  and redemption ... 55, 58-9
  Scriptural authority of ... 16-19, 41
  and self-examination ... 109
  and Spirit of God ... 65-6
  structure of writing ... 56-9, 57n
  trinitarian perspective of ... 56, 58-9, 61-2
Payne, Jon D. ... 26n
Phillips, Richard D. ... 31n
praise for God ... 59-60, 62, 64-5, 66-7, 71
prayer ... 73-4, 77, 74-85, 104-5
present communion ... 28, 37-8, 48-9, 52, 103-4

Rr

redemption ... 18, 37, 54, 55-6, 58-9, 70, 73, 100
Renihan, James M. ... 24n, 94n, 97n, 99n, 100n
Reformation ... 25-6, 25n
Rosner, Brian S. ... 43-4

Ss

sacraments ... 24, 24n, 89-93, 98-101, 106-7
salvation ... 59, 100-1
Savoy Declaration (1658) ... 94
Schaff, Philip ... 89n
Second London Confession of Faith (2nd LCF, 1677/89) ... 16, 21-2, 23, 24, 24n, 93-6
self-examination ... 109-10
sharing ... 33-4, 45-6, 50-2
Sharp, Granville ... 62-3
singing ... 112
spiritual invigoration ... 77, 79, 81
spiritual nourishment ... 22-3, 28, 53, 92, 94-5
... 101, 103, 114
Spurgeon, C. H. ... 53

Tt

table of the Lord............................ 34, 51-2, 99
thankfulness..31-3
Thielman, Frank...80
Thiselton, Anthony..........................46-7, 48-9
three tenses of Lord's Supper 38-9, 113-4

Vv

Vanhoozer, Kevin J. 43n
Vos, Geerhardus................................ 17, 38, 39

Ww

Wallace, Daniel B. 46n, 63n
Weaver, Steve... 114
Westminster Confession of Faith (WCF, 1647) 22, 91-3
Westminster Shorter Catechism (1648)......96
.... 99-101
Willison, John... 108
Wilson, Geoffrey B. 47-10

Zz

Zwingli, Huldrych 26

Scripture Index

Exodus
4:22-23 63
12 37
24:1-11 .... 35-6, 38
34:25 37

Leviticus
9 37

Deuteronomy
16 37
32:17 51

Psalms
28:6 61

Hosea
6:7 63

Matthew
26:26-29 .... 31, 32, 35, 38
26:29 .... 37-8, 39, 113

Mark
14:22-24 .... 31, 32, 35

Luke
3:38 .... 63, 69
14:15 39

John
2:20 80
16:14 .... 70-1, 79
17:17 107

Acts
2:42 33
20:7 33
20:32 107
27:35 33

Romans
1:11 65
8:10 80
15:27 46
15:30-31 83

1 Corinthians
1:9....46, 47, 53
2:14-16....65
8:1-11....42-3
10:1-13....43
10:14....42, 44-5, 51
10:14-22....44
10:16....14, 33-4, 37, 42-3, 45-50,
....53, 70-1, 73, 85, 104, 113
10:18....50
10:19-20....51
10:20-21....45
10:21....34, 51
10:23-33....43
11:17....47
11:20....34
11:23....33
11:23-25....74, 85
11:23-26....31, 32
11:24....37
11:24-25....113
11:26....37-8
11:28....109-10
11:29....113
15:22....69
15:44-46....66

2 Corinthians
1:3....61, 64
1:8-11....83
13:3, 5....80
13:13....47

Galatians
1:18....80
2:20....80

Ephesians
1:3....18, 42, 54, 55-71, 73, 104
1:3-14....55-60
1:4....104
1:7....104
1:8....63, 69
1:15-17....83-5
3:14....18
3:14-21....74-7
3:16-17....42, 54, 85, 104-5
4:15.6....107

Philippians
1:9-11....84

Colossians
1:9....65
1:27....80

1 Timothy
2:5....70

2 Timothy
3:15-17....19

Hebrews
2:10....37

1 Peter
1:3....61, 64
2:2....107
2:5....65
3:18....37

2 Peter
3:15-16....19

Jude
20....107

Revelation
1:10....34-5
19:9....39